TEACHING BASKETBALL

N. Sue Whiddon

University of Florida
Gainesville, Florida

Howard Reynolds

Palm Beach Junior College
Lake Worth, Florida

WAVELAND

PRESS, INC.

Prospect Heights, Illinois

For information about this book, write or call:

Waveland Press, Inc.
P.O. Box 400
Prospect Heights, Illinois 60070
(708) 634-0081

Copyright © 1983 by Macmillan Publishing Company.
Reprinted by arrangement with Macmillan Publishing Company.
1991 reissued by Waveland Press, Inc.

ISBN 0-88133-581-9

Printed in the United States of America

7 6 5 4 3 2 1

Contents

Acknowledgments   v

1 Introduction   1

2 Philosophy and Objectives   3
    Philosophy   3
    Objectives   3
    Projects for Prospective Teachers   5

3 Facilities and Equipment   6
    The Basketball Facility   6
    Recommended Equipment   8
    Modification of Facilities and Equipment   9
    Purchasing   10
    Projects for Prospective Teachers   12

4 Conditioning   13
    Fitness Components   14
    Conditioning for the Competitive Athlete   23
    Projects for Prospective Teachers   27

5 Class Organization   28
    Grouping for Practice   28
    Team Teaching   29
    Instructional Procedures   29
    Coeducational Play   35
    Basketball for Students With Handicaps   37
    Safety   38
    Teaching Aids   38
    Student Leadership   39
    Projects for Prospective Teachers   39

6 Teaching Beginning Skills   40
    Footwork   40
    Handling the Ball   43
    Catching   44
    Passing   45
    Dribbling   48
    Shooting   50
    Rebounding   57
    Individual Defense   59
    Projects for Prospective Teachers   63

7 Teaching Advanced Skills   64
    Advanced Passing Techniques   64
    Advanced Dribbling Skills   69
    Advanced Shooting Skills   72
    Two- and Three-Player Offensive Patterns   74
    Team Offense   77
    Team Defense   85
    Projects for Prospective Teachers   87

8 Lead-ups, Relays, and Modified Games   88
    Lead-up Games   88
    Relays   93
    Modified Games   94
    Projects for Prospective Teachers   96

9 Evaluation   97
    Psychomotor Assessment   97
    Cognitive Assessment   115
    Affective Assessment   118
    Projects for Prospective Teachers   119

10 Coaching Tips   120
    Projects for Prospective Coaches   124

Glossary   125

Annotated Bibliography   127

Index   131

Acknowledgments

We wish to express our sincere appreciation to those who provided materials or assisted in the preparation of this manuscript. This special note of thanks is extended to Linda Blackburn, Suzanne Robinson, Beth Nisco, Jean Dunagan, Barbara Layne, and Ellen Roth.

1

Introduction

Since the inception of basketball at Springfield College in 1891, Dr. Naismith's game has grown tremendously in popular appeal and complexity. Once played with a soccer ball, peach baskets attached to balconies, and a set of 13 original rules, the sport has undergone many changes in its 90-year history. Today the game is played under the jurisdiction of numerous state, national, and international regulatory federations. Basketball appeals equally to men and women participants and provides entertainment for millions of spectators each year. Whether conducted as a backyard pick-up game, physical education unit, varsity sport, recreational activity, or Olympic event, the versatile game offers athletic challenge as well as social and physical benefits to its participants.

Although numerous books have been written on the techniques of playing basketball, the information available on successful teaching of the game is limited. This book is designed to address the specific concerns of prospective or novice teachers, coaches, and recreational leaders. It offers guidance in the areas of player conditioning, class and team organization, teaching skills and strategies, lead-up and modified games, and the evaluation of player and team performance.

The text is organized into ten parts. The first nine chapters contain information appropriate to teaching the beginning or intermediate level player in a school environment. Chapter 2 considers some of the philosophical aspects of teaching and motivating students, enabling them to master skills as well as to achieve personal and social satisfaction in basketball activities. To assist the novice teacher, the chapter includes guidelines for the formulation of performance objectives.

In Chapter 3 we discuss the planning, selection, and purchase of facilities and equipment for class and team use. Chapter 4 describes some of the conditioning activities that can prepare the student for the demands of skill development and game play. Activities suitable for class instruction, as well as those more applicable to a coaching situation, are included.

A realistic approach to effective group organization and instruction is presented in Chapter 5. Also discussed in this section are ways of making the best use of facilities, team teaching, considerations for teaching coeducational and special classes, safety, teaching aids, and student leadership.

The content in Chapters 6 and 7 progresses from acquiring knowledge and skill to applying these competencies to team play. Descriptions of beginning and advanced skills are accompanied by innovative teaching and correctional tips and numerous drills. Recommended sequences for the teaching of specific skills are also provided.

Chapter 8 introduces various lead-up and modified games that can aid skill development in beginning players. Rule changes are suggested that can enhance participation among large groups.

The techniques for assessing individual knowledge and performance that are presented in Chapter 9 may be used to classify students for instruction and to evaluate their progress in meeting predetermined objectives.

The final chapter discusses team selection, conditioning, practice sessions, and other preseasonal and seasonal coaching duties. It is intended to help the novice coach prepare the skilled athlete for competition.

Diagrams and sequential photographs are used throughout the text to depict drill patterns and performance techniques. At the conclusion of each chapter, suggested projects offer the reader a selection of learning activities to reinforce his or her understanding of the material.

The symbols used in the diagrams appear in the legend below. A glossary of terms is at the end of the book.

KEY TO DIAGRAMS

X	Player
⟶	Path of a moving player
⇢	Direction of passed ball
WWWWWWW	Dribble
⊢	Screen or pick
O_1, O_2, O_3, O_4, O_5	Offensive players
D_1, D_2, D_3, D_4, D_5	Defensive players

2

Philosophy and Objectives

PHILOSOPHY

The enjoyment we derive from participating in any sport is enhanced by the improvement in our competence and the consequent increase in our self-esteem. This belief, which many successful teachers and coaches of basketball have reiterated, is further reflected in their emphasis on the mastery of basic skills.

Although teaching styles may vary with the situation, the development of a positive attitude on the part of the teacher or coach as well as the players is fundamental to the learning process. The instructor's attitude toward each class session is likely to be transferred to the students. Similarly, the coach should encourage a positive attitude among the team members; attitude can affect all stages of the team's preparation. To motivate the players most effectively, teachers and coaches should not overlook the importance of combining an element of fun with the development of skill.

A combination of good organization and challenging activities is the key to motivating students in the development of isolated skills. If learning activities are selected without proper planning and instructional sequences are conducted in a haphazard manner, students will not benefit from them. Both the teacher and the student should determine immediate and long-range goals. Throughout the learning process, students should be encouraged to keep their chosen goals in mind. Demands and expectations should be reasonably attainable, and students must understand their individual roles and responsibilities. As progress is made, establishing new activities, challenges, and higher goals for physical and emotional growth should be a continuous process for individual students and for the class in general. This "overload principle" prevents students from being completely satisfied with previous levels of achievement and makes skill practice a desirable alternative to play. The desired result of overload is change: more specifically, improvement in skill and attitude. The same principle can be applied to coaching skilled athletes on interscholastic teams, although the expectations undoubtedly will be greater.

OBJECTIVES

The initial step in planning any basketball program is to determine appropriate goals on which subsequent content and evaluation will be based. To ensure that the student understands the desired performance outcomes of the basketball unit, standards should be established and expressed in written performance objectives.

Performance (behavioral) objectives must specify conditions for evaluation, state minimum levels of acceptable performance, and be measurable. Stated in terms of observable behavior, the following objective clearly tells the student what must be done and gives the standard for satisfactory completion of the skill: *The student will be able to dribble a ball the length of the floor in 10 sec without committing a violation.* Using the same skill task, standards may be altered to meet the skill level and experience of the class. For example, the expectations for the beginning level student in the objective just cited could be increased for intermediate students by decreasing the maximum time allowance to 8 sec.

Performance tasks should be applicable to various age, sex, and experience levels in the program. Thus, both the unskilled beginning player and the highly skilled experienced athlete will be challenged by the expectations for their particular levels.

Measurable standards offer the teacher and student an objective basis for the evaluation of skill and progress. For evaluative and motivational purposes, specific performance expectations may be designated for each division within the grading system. For instance, standards may be established for "A" level performance, "B" level, and so forth. Performance expectations can be determined by using national norms such as those presented in Chapter 9. In establishing separate performance standards for various age groups, the instructor should use the norms for each age at selected percentile levels. When students within the same age group are organized into different skill classifications, performance standards for each skill level may be determined by using the norms at different percentiles for that age group. For example, norms at the 75th percentile may be suitable as standards for advanced students; norms at the 50th percentile may be more suitable as minimal performance standards for beginning students.

Care should be taken to develop performance objectives that emphasize competencies necessary for successful performance. According to Annarino's taxonomy (Annarino 1977), objectives in physical education may be categorized into four major domains: physical, psychomotor, cognitive, and affective. The physical domain concerns the organic development of the body systems to meet the demands of the activity, including strength, endurance, and flexibility. Perceptual motor and fundamental movement skill objectives are representative of the psychomotor domain. Objectives in the cognitive domain concern the intellectual development of the student: acquiring and applying knowledge of rules, strategies, etiquette, terminology, and body functions. The final category deals with the social and emotional development of the student, including responses to activity, self-actualization, and self-esteem. Sample performance objectives for each domain are listed below.

Physical Objectives

As a result of participation in this unit, the student will:

1. Demonstrate a high level of cardiovascular endurance by running/walking a distance of 1.75 mi (boys) or 1.2 mi (girls) in 12 min.
2. Demonstrate sufficient arm strength by executing eight pull-ups (boys), or hanging in a flexed-arm position for 40 sec (girls).

Psychomotor Objectives

As a result of participation in this unit, the student will:

1. Complete five chest passes against wall from a distance of 9 ft within 10 sec.
2. Legally dribble a ball the length of the court within 10 sec, using the nondominant hand.

Cognitive Objectives

As a result of participation in this unit, the student will:

1. Attain a minimum score of 85 percent correct on a written examination on the rules of basketball.
2. Correctly identify in writing the penalties imposed for designated infractions of the rules.

Affective Objectives

As a result of participation in this unit, the student will:

1. Demonstrate sportsmanship by accepting all judgment decisions of officials in a controlled manner.
2. Demonstrate a desire to work effectively with others to achieve group goals, by participating in offensive and defensive teamwork.

PROJECTS FOR PROSPECTIVE TEACHERS

1. Write a sample objective for each of the four domains: physical, psychomotor, cognitive, and affective. Use information in Chapter 9 to determine suitable standards of performance for a beginning junior high school class in basketball.
2. Visit a local junior high school and senior high school to discuss appropriate performance objectives with the physical education teacher. Compare the performance objectives designated for students on each of the two levels.

Reference

Annarino, A. "Physical Education Objectives." *JOPERD* 48(1977):22.

3

Facilities and Equipment

THE BASKETBALL FACILITY

Dimensions

A regulation court for the game of basketball measures 50 × 94 ft. The National Federation of State High School Athletic Associations advocates that high school competition be conducted on a court with dimensions of no less than 50 × 84 ft (NFSHSAA 1979). A minimum of 6 ft of out-of-bounds space with an overhead clearance of 22 ft is highly recommended. In small gymnasiums where end lines are close to the walls, mats can be hung to lessen the impact of players colliding with the walls. The sides and bottom of the backboards, basket standards, and any obstructions within 6 ft of the court should be similarly padded to prevent injury.

Figure 3.1 shows the court layout and regulation dimensions. Additional floor and wall space at the ends of the playing courts may be created by retracting the bleachers. This space is invaluable for drill practice and skill testing. For class and recreational purposes, a greater number of players may be accommodated if two or more courts are laid out across the regulation court area. For width-wise play, retractable side baskets or portable baskets may be used for goals. To distinguish between courts, lines should be painted a color that contrasts with other regulation court markings.

Court Surfaces

Court surfaces vary from the traditional wood flooring to the more contemporary synthetic surfaces. The most popular hardwood flooring is northern maple that is a minimum 25/32 in. thick. Parquet squares have been found to be less expensive and more practical for school settings. Care must be taken to avoid dampness, and water should not be left standing on the floor; excessive moisture may cause the wood to buckle. After installment and sanding, two sealer coats should be applied to protect the wood from moisture. Lines are then painted and the final coats of gym seal applied. To enhance their visibility, the out-of-bounds area, center circle, and free throw lanes may be painted a color that contrasts with the playing court.

Because synthetic flooring has a greater, more even resilience than wood flooring, it allows for a more uniform ball bounce and better sound absorption. Another advantage of synthetic flooring is that the number of certain athletic injuries, including shin splints, may be reduced. On the other hand, floor burns may be more severe than those that result from sliding on wood flooring. Varying

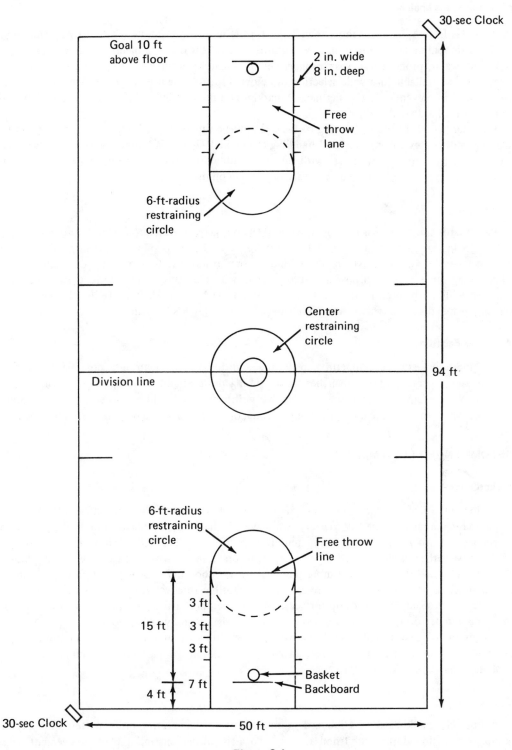

Figure 3.1
Basketball court diagram shows permanent lines

in thickness from 1/16 in. to more than 1 in., synthetic flooring can be repaired by cutting and re-placing damaged areas. In addition, most authorities confirm that nonflammable surfaces are not af-fected by water, produce less wear on shoes and balls, and are less subject to abuse from street shoes. They are also available in a wide selection of colors. Tape may be used for court lines, and can easily be removed to prevent excessive permanent markings on the multipurpose courts. Price is comparable to that of the hardwood surface.

Like hardwood, synthetic playing surfaces should be dust-mopped daily to protect players from slipping and to prevent impaired ball handling (Penman 1977). In addition, synthetic surface manu-facturers suggest weekly washings with an autoscrubber for quality maintenance. Both floorings require some type of refinishing at intervals, depending on use.

Backboards

Backboards must be of a flat, rigid material (wood, glass, synthetic, or metal), either fan-shaped (54 X 35 in.) or rectangular (6 X 4 ft), and supported by floor standards or suspended from the ceiling. Portable, adjustable standards for indoor or outdoor use with 8–10-ft adjustable posts and wheels may serve a dual purpose as net-game standards. On transparent boards, the basket may be centered within a painted rectangle. Attached to each backboard, 10 ft above the playing surface, is the orange metal goal to which a cord or chain (all-weather) net is looped.

Auxiliary Facilities

For interscholastic or competitive play, the addition of an electronic scoreboard, retractable bleachers for spectators, team benches, horn, timing devices, and a loudspeaker system is recom-mended. When team possession rules apply, two visible clocks should be placed at opposite ends of the floor where the end line meets the right sideline, or displayed above or behind each backboard.

RECOMMENDED EQUIPMENT

Basketballs

Various pieces of standard equipment are necessary to conduct a class unit in basketball properly. In purchasing, a ratio of one ball to every two players is the suggested rule of thumb. Basketballs may be rubber or leather, with a maximum circumference of 29.5–30 in. and weighing between 20 and 22 oz. Quality leather balls are relatively expensive; to preserve the covers, these should be used only in the gymnasium. Rubber balls are more practical for outdoor and class use, and cost approximately half as much as leather balls. They are also less susceptible to cover tears on rough surfaces, and are not affected by contact with damp surfaces. "Weather leather" balls are made of a synthetic material that feels and performs like leather but is more scuff resistant and weatherproof.

During the off-season, balls should be wiped clean with soap and water, and a conditioner should be applied to the leather. For storage, all basketballs should be partially deflated and placed in a cool, dry area.

Chalkboard

A portable chalkboard or clipboard is convenient for illustrating drills, patterns of play, and group organization during discussion sessions. To assist in demonstrating player movement, several manufacturers design their chalkboards to include a reverse-side magnetic board with court diagrams and small magnetized objects denoting the players and ball.

Ball Carriers and Cones or Chairs

Six mesh ball carriers or two racks are necessary to transport equipment to and from the equipment room. In addition, a minimum of six cones or chairs are recommended, primarily for skill testing and drills.

Apparel

Pinnies may be cotton or plastic, with clearly visible numbers on the front and back. Although more expensive jerseys may be worn for interscholastic games, pinnies suffice for class purposes. To prevent confusion on the court and add to team cohesiveness, each individual participating as a player or substitute should have an article of team identification as part of his or her standard attire. Cloth pinnies, jerseys, and officials' shirts must be laundered regularly. Plastic pinnies are easy to maintain and may be wiped off after each wearing.

Personal apparel includes properly fitted basketball shoes with good cushion, arch support, and suction soles. Students with weak ankles may prefer high-top shoes for additional support. Two pairs of clean, heavy socks should be worn to prevent blisters and absorb perspiration. Guards or holders should be available for students who wear glasses. Uniforms should be lightweight, require little care, and allow freedom of movement.

Supplementary Equipment for Competitive Teams

Supplementary equipment appropriate for skilled athletes in competitive programs is listed below.

1. Rebounders, which elevate the ball to a height of 8-12 ft, can be used to develop vertical jumping ability and strengthen hands and forearms. They may be purchased with a permanent or rolling base and height gauges.
2. A set of 17-in. practice rings, which install over the regulation 18-in. goals, improves shooting accuracy by requiring increased concentration during practice.
3. Breakaway rims are reflex rims that release at approximately 230 lb of pressure. A spring-loaded latch automatically returns the rim to the original play position. Approved by the National Collegiate Athletic Association and National Federation of High Schools, this device helps minimize the number of bent rims, shattered glass backboards, game interruptions, associated injuries, and costly repairs and replacements.
4. Medicine balls help to develop upper arm and shoulder strength and eye coordination. Teachers may wish to use this equipment in class as well as team practice.
5. Ankle weights and weighted vests may be worn during practice and running drills; they help to strengthen leg muscles and promote jumping ability.
6. Dribbling glasses, which block lower vision, encourage touch control of the dribble instead of visual control.

MODIFICATION OF FACILITIES AND EQUIPMENT

Considerations for Beginners

For participants in upper elementary, middle, or junior high school, certain modifications of the game, including proportionate reductions in the height of the goal, court dimensions, and the circumference of the ball, may improve performance.

The appropriateness of one basket height for all ages and levels of players is not a new issue. As early as 1931, suggestions were made at a meeting of the National Association of Basketball Coaches to elevate baskets to 12 ft for college and professional play (Henry 1979). Since that date, attempts have been made to overcome the advantage of tall players through modifications in rules rather than changes in facilities. Insufficient evidence is available to allow us to make judgments about the relationship of basket height to development of shooting skill in children. Numerous authorities on elementary physical education, however, suggest that adapting the game and basket heights for young children promotes the initial development of fundamental techniques and the student's eventual realization of success. Although lowered baskets in gymnasiums are presently uncommon, many elementary school playgrounds have hard court surfaces with baskets at 8 or 9 ft. For indoor or outdoor use, adjustable basketball backstops, which may be set at any height from 0 to 10 ft, may be purchased or made.

Smaller courts may be designed for younger participants, to prevent excessive fatigue and limit the space required for the game. When portable standards are used, court dimensions can be reduced to 42 × 74 ft without inhibiting play. Crosscourt games using side baskets are also recommended. Other dimensions, including the distance from a free throw line to the basket, may be reduced to increase shooting success.

Junior or Biddy basketballs, with a circumference of 28 in. and a weight of 18 oz, are designed for the small hands and limited strength of young participants. Because the smaller ball enhances ball handling, passing, and shooting ability, the game or lead-up game can be made more enjoyable for the child. Small rubber playground balls may supplement the junior ball inventory, enabling each child to have access to a ball in skill development activities. To enlarge the shooting target, hula hoops may be hung from the basket. Any ball passing through the hoop counts as a score.

Goal Reinforcer

Unsupervised outdoor baskets are often damaged by players grasping the rims. With the advent of the dunk shot, goals are often bent. "Super goals," consisting of a double ring and double bracing, have been marketed as the strongest goals available. The addition of a metal piece to reinforce existing goals may also relieve the problem of damage. Anyone with welding knowledge could provide the necessary expertise, using the following instructions (Hinga 1978): Using a 24 × 4 in. piece of #12 gauge plate, cut it on a diagonal into two 3.5 × 24 in. triangles (Figure 3.2a). Weld the larger end of each triangle to a side of the back brace of the goal (Figure 3.2b). Bend the metal around the sides of the rim. The top of the metal pieces should be level with and reinforce the goal.

PURCHASING

The basketball teacher or coach undoubtedly has some responsibility in selecting or purchasing equipment. In purchasing, the following general tips may be kept in mind:

1. Methodically plan purchases over several years, especially expensive items such as balls and uniforms. This eliminates the need for excessive costs in a particular year, maintains the inventory, and demonstrates consistency in budget requisitioning.
2. Base purchases on needs determined through accurate inventories.
3. Purchase in the spring for a fall basketball program. This assures early delivery and receipt of any special requests.

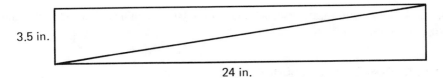

Figure 3.2a
Metal brace

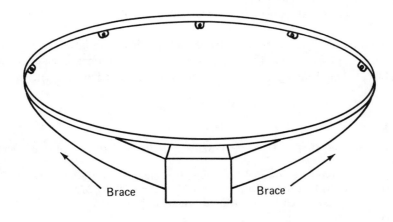

Figure 3.2b
Back view

Figure 3.2
Goal reinforcer

4. Beware of making bargain purchases without knowledge of the equipment's quality. Middle-priced equipment generally provides acceptable performance and durability for class purposes.
5. Consider available discounts, as long as quality is not sacrificed. Early purchasing, prompt payment of bills, ordering in quantity, and special discounts can result in savings. Balls with minor cover blemishes can often be purchased for half the cost of perfect ones.
6. Before purchasing, request samples of new equipment or styles recommended by the vendor.
7. Purchase from reputable firms and manufacturers who guarantee their products. Because they offer especially good service, local dealers should be used as long as their prices are comparable to those offered from other sources.
8. Purchase from several manufacturers who specialize in certain items; this may assure the best quality equipment (Cooper 1975).

9. Check invoices as deliveries are made, and return faulty equipment for refund. Maintain accurate purchase records.

PROJECTS FOR PROSPECTIVE TEACHERS

1. Observe a maintenance crew making preseason preparation of a basketball floor. Describe the step-by-step procedure.
2. Review three different equipment catalogs, comparing prices and quality of equipment that would be desirable for class purposes.
3. Describe the care and storage of basketball equipment in a high school physical education program.
4. Review literature on different types of basketball flooring, then interview a facilities manager or chairman of a physical education department. Request information on prices, maintenance, and durability of hardwood and synthetic court surfaces, and submit a written report on your findings.

References

Cooper, J., and Siedentop, D. *The Theory and Science of Basketball*. 2nd ed. Philadelphia: Lea and Febiger, 1975.

Henry, G. "Should the Basket Be Lowered for Young Participants?" *JOPERD* 50(1979):66.

Hinga, J. "Rugged Basketball Goals for Outdoors." *JOPERD* 49(1978):27.

National Federation of State High School Athletic Associations. *1980 Basketball Rule Book*. Elgin, Ill.: NFSHSAA, 1979.

Penman, K. *Planning Physical Education and Athletic Facilities in Schools*. New York: John Wiley and Sons, 1977.

4

Conditioning

Fitness for the game of basketball refers to the player's ability to (1) perform at high speeds for extended periods of time without extreme signs of fatigue and (2) recuperate quickly during breaks.

Basketball teachers and coaches recognize the reduced possibility of injuries as an advantage associated with player fitness. Physicians have attributed 60 percent of all basketball injuries to improper mental and physical conditioning (Barnes 1973). Later in this chapter, specific conditioning techniques that are appropriate for competitive teams will be described.

Basketball instructors are frequently confronted with students who are unfit for the physical demands of the game. Because the class time available for both conditioning and skill teaching is usually limited, emphasis on fitness for the activity is often insufficient.

The physical educator has numerous options in dealing with the practical difficulties of conditioning students. A few suggested methods follow.

1. Immediately preceding the unit on basketball, conduct a unit on body conditioning and weight training or on a sport activity that develops the desired fitness components.
2. Schedule basketball skill activities and body conditioning on alternate days of the week.
3. Use flexible scheduling throughout the school to provide extended class periods and sufficient time for skill and fitness development.
4. Select drills and group activities that simultaneously improve skill and promote conditioning.
5. As an integral beginning to each class session, apply circuit training that includes skill and fitness stations as well as mandatory jogging between stations.
6. Incorporate exercises and jogging during the class period.

Although the expectations of the coach or teacher may vary from class to team players, one basic premise of conditioning applies to both teaching and coaching: the teacher or coach must gradually increase the work load of the participants until a desired level of fitness is attained. This level is subsequently maintained primarily through demanding class activities or practices and games. The work load may be increased by increasing either the extent of work or the intensity of work (the amount done in a set time). For example, time used for game play could gradually be lengthened to increase the work. The intensity of the class or practice session could be increased by having students perform more demanding drills.

FITNESS COMPONENTS

Certain components of fitness, including cardiorespiratory and muscular endurance, arm and leg strength, body flexibility, and agility, are necessary complements to the acquisition of skills.

Cardiorespiratory Endurance Conditioning

Cardiorespiratory endurance is required for prolonged activity that places continuous stress on the circulatory and respiratory systems. When the overload principle is applied, the following activities have been found to be effective in the development of cardiorespiratory endurance:

1. Running stairs in a stadium or gymnasium. To enable the student to progress in the conditioning process, length of running time or the number of stairs climbed within a set time should be increased.
2. Jumping rope or jumping in place (ten short jumps, then ten high jumps).
3. Running sprints. To motivate students, 50-yd sprints should be run in groups of two or more. Increasing the number or length of sprints increases work load.
4. Jumping over a bench approximately 16 in. high 20 consecutive times. To increase the conditioning effect, a second set may be added after a 1-min rest.
5. Running cross-country: jogging over a variety of terrains, beginning with short distances and building up to 2 or 3 mi. Parcours running is also recommended.
6. Six-player passing drill.

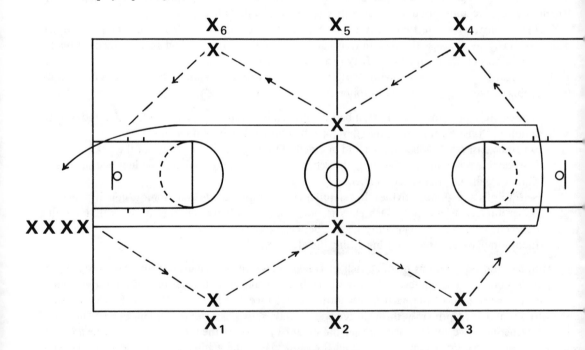

Figure 4.1
Six-player passing drill

- Six players are stationed around the court as shown in Figure 4.1.
- Other players, each with a ball, line up single file behind the end line.
- The first player in line passes the ball to the sideline player (X_1) and breaks to half court.
- After passing the foul line, the first player receives a return pass and passes to the closest center circle player (X_2).
- The pass is returned as the breaking player reaches half court.
- The player passes on the run to the sideline player (X_3), receives a return pass, and shoots a lay-up.
- Rebounding the ball, the player rapidly repeats the process down the opposite sideline.
- After completing the last lay-up, the player returns to the end of the player line.
- The second player in line begins the process at the first player crosses center court for the first time.

Muscular Endurance Conditioning

Muscular endurance determines the extent to which repeated contractions can be made without the muscle succumbing to fatigue. To prepare for running an average distance of 3 mi in the course of a game, players need to develop muscular endurance in the legs. The arms must be similarly conditioned to sustain frequent use and being held in an upright position for long periods. Drills recommended for increasing muscular endurance include:

Touch-and-Go Drill (Figure 4.2)

Each student:

- Starts at end line
- Sprints to foul line
- Pivots and returns to end line
- Pivots and sprints to half court
- Sprints to opposite foul line
- Pivots and returns to end line
- Sprints to farthest end line
- Pivots and returns to starting end line

For expediency and to add a competitive element, several students may run this drill simultaneously.

Zigzag Drill (Figure 4.3)

The zigzag drill helps strengthen legs.

- In single file, students start at the left corner of the court behind the end line, and run the length of the court, zigzagging with sharp cutting movements.
- After crossing the end line, students run backward to the opposite sideline, assume a low defensive position, and slide the length of the court in a zigzag pattern without crossing feet.
- Return to starting line and repeat.

Continuous Lay-ups (Figure 4.4)

Executing continuous lay-ups helps develop leg and arm strength.

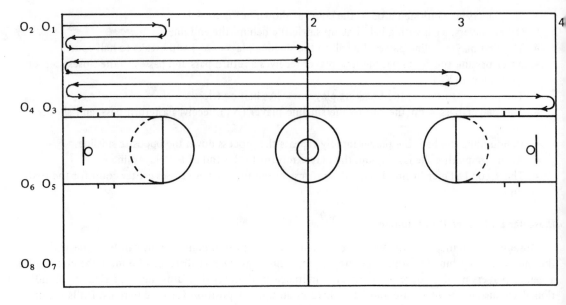

Figure 4.2
Touch-and-go drill

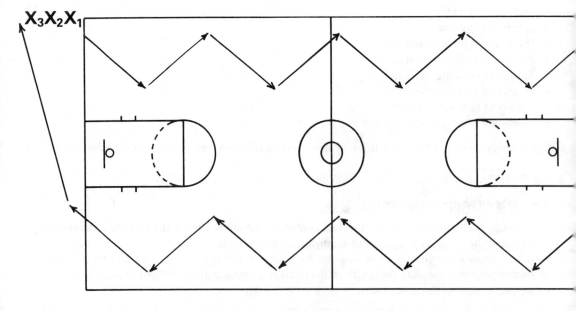

Figure 4.3
Zigzag drill

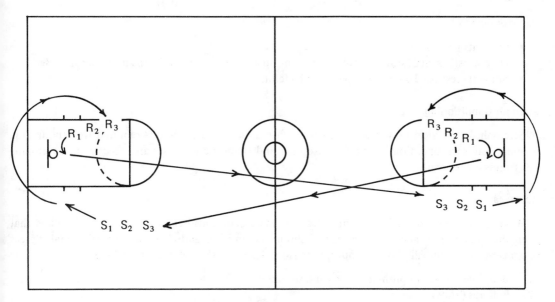

Figure 4.4
Continuous lay-ups (S, shooting player; R, rebounding player)

- Players form two lines at each end basket. One line shoots lay-ups, and the other line takes rebounds.
- After taking a lay-up, players move to the rebounding line at that end of the court.
- After rebounding, players move to the shooting line at the opposite basket.
- Players progress to the rebounding line and back to the original shooting line at the opposite end of the court. Lines should be kept short (three or four players), requiring students to move constantly. A set number of continuous lay-ups may be required for completion of the drill. To increase work load, allot more time for the drill or shorten the lines to increase the pace.

Defensive Drill

The defensive drill is another way of working on leg and arm strength.

- In an open military formation, students spread across the central area of the court, face the instructor, and assume a defensive position to await the instructor's signal.
- On hand signals from the instructor, students quickly slide right, left, up, or back, until the whistle blows. At the sound of the whistle, students stutter step as rapidly as possible until another hand signal is given.
- In one variation, students stutter step and rotate a quarter turn on each of four consecutive whistles until they face the instructor.
- In another variation, students make a half turn on each stutter rotation, and a full turn on the final stutter.
- Continue drill for approximately 2 min. To increase the conditioning effect, progressively lengthen drill time.

Rapid Jumps

- Students form a circle.
- On a whistle signal, students hold their arms up and execute rapid jumps in place for 15 sec.
- Students rest for 10 sec and repeat five to ten times.

Strength Conditioning

Strength, or physical power generated through muscular contraction, is required for rebounding, jumping, and sprinting. Combinations of isotonic and isometric exercises are effective in developing this fitness component.

Isotonics

When performed correctly and progressively increased, calisthenics are isotonic exercises that strengthen the fingers and hands, arms and shoulders, and legs and abdominal muscles, major areas of concern for basketball players. Appropriate isotonics for basketball players include:

1. Bent-knee fingertip push-ups (arms and shoulders)
2. Pull-ups (arms)
3. Bent-knee sit-ups (abdomen)
4. Bench step-ups or Harvard Step Test (legs)
5. Squat jumps (legs). From a half-squat position, students jump upward until the body is fully extended, then return to a half-squat position.
6. Continuous jumps to touch backboard (muscular endurance for legs and arms). Student is stationed under the basket, slightly to the left or right of the rim. With arms extended, student attempts to touch the backboard. Student repeats the action a set number of times or for a set time period.
7. Rubber ball squeezing (hands and arms)
8. Vigorous hand waving (hands and forearms)
9. Jumping rope (legs, coordination, and endurance)
10. Toe raises (legs). Student raises heels from the floor, stands on toes, then lowers heels without allowing them to touch the floor. Action is repeated several times.
11. Tuck jumps (legs). Student stands with feet together, then jumps as high as possible, tucking knees to chest and grasping knees momentarily with hands. Action is repeated ten times.
12. Ankle walk (ankles). Student walks around gym, placing body weight on the outside of the feet.
13. Toe drawing (feet). Student places a pencil between toes and attempts to draw large circles on a piece of paper on the floor.
14. Ankle extension (ankles). Student sits with legs extended and flexes ankles, attempting to point toes upward while a partner provides resistance with hands on top of student's feet. Student then moves toes downward from the flexed upward position while partner provides resistance on the balls of the feet. When the resistance is sufficient to make the feet immovable, the exercise becomes isometric; effort in that direction should be sustained for approximately 8 sec.

Isometrics

Although muscular endurance and flexibility are more effectively developed through isotonic exercise, isometrics are beneficial in building strength. Performed individually or with a partner, isometrics require maximum muscular effort exerted against an immovable resistance for 8–10 sec.

The individual student may perform isometrics by placing a rolled towel at the nape of the neck, the lumbar region of the back, or under the foot. The student grasps both ends of the towel, and pulls forward or upward as the body part resists.

Combined with isotonic exercise, the following dual isometrics are recommended as preseason strength conditioners (Ortwerth 1972):

1. Bird-up

    - Student kneels with elbows extended at shoulder height, arms flexed, and hands under chin.
    - Partner places hands on top of the elbows, and pushes downward while student resists.

2. Bird-down

    - Student assumes bird-up starting position.
    - Partner places hands under the elbows, and pulls upward while student resists.

3. Curl-ups

    - With fingers interlaced behind head, student assumes bent-knee sit-up position.
    - Student attempts to curl head and shoulder blades off the floor, while partner pushes downward with one hand on the student's chest and the other hand holding down the feet.

4. Leg press

    - Student lies on back under a horizontal bar lowered to a height of 3–3.5 ft.
    - With legs bent, student pushes up on the bar with the feet.

Weight Training

Weight training and resistance exercises can be an excellent source of strength development. As mentioned earlier, this training may be offered prior to or on alternate days with the basketball unit. Athletes participating in a competitive program generally engage more extensively and intensively in these activities, including an off-season program. For this reason, exercises using free weights and resistive equipment are discussed under the heading "Conditioning for the Competitive Athlete."

Flexibility Conditioning

Flexibility refers to the range of motion of various body parts and is required to perform the twisting, stretching, and bending actions during a game. All class or team warm-ups should begin with stretching exercises. A gradual stretching of various muscle groups contributes to effective movement and lessens the possibility of muscle and tendon damage caused by overstretching (elongation of the fibers).

To obtain the maximum effect from the performance of flexibility exercises, proper technique is mandatory. When the range of motion is limited in any joint, forcing a stretch by bouncing may cause damage to muscle, ligament, or cartilage. The body part should be moved slowly through its range of motion until the threshold of pain is reached. This position is then maintained 5–8 sec, released, and repeated. The range of motion should gradually be increased.

The following flexibility exercises are recommended for basketball players:

1. Body bender (torso)

    - With fingers interlaced behind head, bend sideward to the left.
    - Return to starting position and bend to the right.

2.   Knee-to-head stretch (back and legs)

- With weight on hands and knees, bring right knee up to touch dropped head.
- Return to starting position.
- Reverse procedure by bringing left knee to head and returning to starting position.

3.   Achilles stretch (calf muscles)

- Standing at arm's length from the wall, lean forward until the head touches the wall, with arms supporting weight. Heels must remain on the floor.
- Return to starting position by extending arms. (To increase shoulder and arm strength, wall push-ups may also be done from this position.)

4.   Stride stretch (legs)

- From a squatting position, fully extend left leg out to side.
- Rock weight over the extended leg.
- Return to starting position and reverse leg positions.

5.   Hamstring stretch (legs)

- Standing with the legs crossed at the feet, bend forward at the waist and lower hands to the floor.
- Return to starting position and slowly repeat.

6.   Bench stretch (legs and back)

- Stand, facing a bench with one leg extended, resting the heel on the bench.
- Grasp the ankle of the extended leg with both hands and bend forward, placing chest on the leg.
- Switch leg positions.

7.   Pretzel bend (back)

- Lying flat on the back with arms close to the body, lift legs over the head, touching toes to the floor.
- Throughout the exercise, keep legs straight, and palms in contact with the floor.

8.   Chest and thigh lift (abdomen and legs)

- From a prone position and with arms at sides, lift head and shoulders off the floor and hold for 5 sec.
- Return to prone position.
- Lift legs upward approximately 1 ft off the floor and hold for 5 sec.

9.   Arm circles (arms)

- Stand with arms extended outward at shoulder level, palms down.
- Circle the arms forward, then backward, gradually increasing the radius of each circle.

Static Stretching

Static stretching, resistive exercises that increase the range of motion and reduce the likelihood of muscle and tendon pulls, involves activities with a partner that can be incorporated into the conditioning or warm-up phase of the class. Students must be cautioned against forcing a partner to stretch beyond his or her individual limits. The following exercise uses static stretching and is considered appropriate for basketball players:

1. With palms out, student stretches straight arms as far behind body as possible, pushing shoulder blades together.
2. Partner grasps the student's arms at the elbows and offers resistance as the student attempts to pull the arms forward.
3. Student again moves arms back as far as possible. This time the backs of the hands should be closer together.
4. To adapt the process for the legs and back, the student lifts upward from a prone position as resistance is applied.

Agility Conditioning

Agility may be defined as nimbleness, balance, and quickness in changing direction. In basketball, agility enables a player to maneuver offensively, adjust defensively, and make the transition from offense to defense. The following movements and exercises can contribute to the development of agility:

1. Jumping rope
2. Sprinting, stopping, sprinting
3. Running backward around the perimeter of the court
4. Directional shuffle. Using sliding steps, student changes direction at a signal from the teacher.
5. Shuttle running or touch-and-go drill
6. Agility box

   - A 3 X 2 ft box is chalked or taped on the floor with a line dividing the box lengthwise.
   - A student straddles the division line. As rapidly as possible, he or she jumps with both feet into the right and then the left half of the box.
   - The student continues jumping from one half to the other as rapidly as possible for the designated duration of the drill.

7. Bench jumping. Student stands with one side facing a bench or box and jumps over and back 20 times.
8. One-foot hop. Student hops on one foot around the perimeter of the court. Exercise is then repeated on the other foot.
9. Agility jumps

   - One student assumes a hands-and-knees position on the floor.
   - A second student stands to the side of the kneeling student, facing in the same direction.
   - The second student jumps with both feet over the back of the first student and assumes a hands-and-knees position.
   - The first student then jumps over the second student, and the exercise continues for a specific number of jumps, length of time, or distance down the floor.

10. Agility jumps may be performed by three or more students in an agility chain. To make an agility chain:

    - Each student assumes a hands-and-knees position on the floor, with the head near the feet of the student in front.

- One student begins the process by jumping from side to side over the backs of the other students, starting with the person at the end of the chain. The student continues jumping over subsequent students until reaching the front of the line.
- The jumper then assumes a hands-and-knees position, and the last player in the line becomes the jumper.

11. The maze

   - Starting behind the end line, the student sprints along the right sideline to half court, assumes a defensive position, and slides laterally to the left sideline.
   - Student runs backward to the opposite end line and slides to the right sideline.

12. Agility drill (see defensive drill described earlier for developing muscular endurance).
13. Signal drill (variation of defensive drill)

   - All students line up on the end line, facing the instructor.
   - The instructor gives verbal signals designating specific locomotor movements (jog, slide, hop) and hand signals indicating direction. Emphasis is on quick changes of direction.

14. Shuffle box

   - A shuffle box approximately 10 × 10 ft is drawn on the floor.
   - Starting at the back of the box, student uses sliding steps to move quickly forward, back to center, side to side, back to center, and out the front, touching all lines. Students may be timed.

15. Slide and sprint drill

   - Students line up along the end line, face the right sideline, and assume a defensive stance.
   - On signal, students slide down the length of the floor and sprint back.
   - Backward running may be substituted for the sprint.

Circuit Training

Fundamental skills and conditioning can be improved simultaneously by using circuit stations at the beginning or end of class or practice sessions. Once instructed about the organization of the circuit, students begin at an assigned station and rotate from station to station, either as a group on whistle command or individually at their own pace. Drills or exercises may be performed at each location for a fixed time period or number of repetitions. Stations are numbered to make rotation easier, and students should be instructed to run from station to station. As the conditioning level of the students improves, the number of repetitions may be increased, or more intense drills may be added or substituted. The entire circuit should take approximately 15 min to complete. If the circuit is to be effective, all students must demonstrate 100 percent effort and self-discipline.

When planning a circuit, the instructor should not arrange drills or exercises that work the same area of the body in succession. A good sequence will enable one muscle group to recover while other body parts are placed under stress. Students should be encouraged to put forth their best effort at each station. One way to motivate students and to make the station activities more enjoyable is to accompany circuit training with upbeat music that appeals to the students. Performing to a musical beat may also help students make their movements more rhythmic.

A few activities appropriate for circuit stations include:

1. Rope jumping (50 jumps on each foot and 50 jumps on both)
2. Calisthenics (bent-leg sit-ups, squat thrusts, push-ups, and others)
3. Obstacle dribble. Student weaves in and out of a row of six cones or chairs as rapidly as possible, changing hands as each obstacle is approached.
4. Bench jumping (20 times)
5. Alternate lay-ups. Student is positioned under basket, and alternates shooting right- and left-handed lay-ups as rapidly as possible for a set time. Student immediately shifts to the opposite side of the basket after each attempt, successful or not.
6. Sliding across the lane

    • Starting at one of the free throw lane lines, the student assumes a defensive stance, with his or her back to the basket.
    • The student moves from lane line to lane line ten times, moving as quickly as possible and touching the floor outside each line with the hand. (As in shuffle box drill, students may be timed.)

7. Speed dribbling. At top speed, student dribbles the length of the floor using the nondominant hand.
8. Dribble steal. Each student dribbles and maintains control of a ball while attempting to make another student lose control of the ball.
9. Touch-and-go running drill (see above, under "Muscular Endurance Conditioning")
10. Wall rebounding

    • Students line up single file, facing a wall.
    • The first student tosses a ball upward against the wall and moves quickly to the end of the line.
    • Each subsequent student jumps to rebound and tosses or taps the ball against the wall.
    • After touching the ball, students move quickly to the end of the line.

CONDITIONING FOR THE COMPETITIVE ATHLETE

The same principles of increased work load used in classroom situations also apply to conditioning the skilled athlete for competition. The coach's performance expectations must continue to challenge each player: conditioning should not be restricted to a few weeks of preseason activities. Instead, players should acquire and maintain fitness through a progressive, multiseasonal program.

Off-season

Many coaches believe that an off-season program that develops the desired level of strength, endurance, and flexibility is the winning edge. If weight training is used twice weekly to improve strength, care should be taken to tailor the program to each individual with regard to the amount to be lifted, number of repetitions, and number of sets. Because upper body and leg strength are of utmost importance to basketball players, these areas should receive the greatest attention in planning the weight program. Female players can benefit from improved muscle tone and strength without fear of becoming muscle-bound. If access to a weight room cannot be obtained, an alternative exercise program should be required. Suggested exercises might include sit-ups, push-ups, leg lifts, rocking chairs, and rope jumping.

Because of the nature of the game, off-season conditioning should include both distance running (working up to 2–3 mi) and sprint running to develop speed and endurance. Each player should maintain a daily progress chart, including distances, times, and body weight, and submit it to the coach at the first practice. Daily free throw shooting is recommended, and may also be charted for improvement.

Preseason

Most conditioning work is preseasonal (six to eight weeks' formal practice) and during the first two to three weeks of the season (Moore and White 1980). Preseason conditioning should be structured to develop cardiorespiratory endurance, quickness, and speed, through short-distance running (repeated sprints), running in place, and interval training. Preliminary warm-ups should be a part of each workout. Muscle strength, flexibility, and endurance may be improved by applying the overload principle to a program consisting of (1) isotonic and isometric exercises designed for specific muscles and (2) weight training (three times a week) (Ortwerth 1972). To increase agility, running should include forward, backward, and lateral movements. Informal one-on-one, two-on-two, or half-court play may follow the conditioning work. A sample preseason program is shown in Table 4.1.

In-season

During the season, conditioning will consist of running, participating in demanding practice sessions, and a continuous weight training program. When players are tired at the end of practice or class, running drills may be effective for conditioning (e.g., running stairs and wind sprints).

Practices should vary in physical difficulty, with no more than three strenuous practices in a row. During strenuous sessions, players are pushed to their physical limit, and all drills are primarily designed for conditioning purposes. Heavy workout days may be alternated with lighter workout days that focus on less fatiguing skill drills (individual work, game situations, or half-court scrimmages) (Ortwerth 1972). The in-season weight training program should continue three times a week, emphasizing upper and lower body development on alternate days.

Table 4.1
Sample Preseason Program

Monday	Tuesday	Wednesday	Thursday	Friday
Warm-ups	Warm-ups	Warm-ups	Warm-ups	Warm-ups
Weight training	Circuit training	Weight training	Circuit training	Weight training
Offensive or defensive practice	Free throws	Offensive or defensive practice	Free throws	Offensive or defensive practice
Sprints	Passing, shooting, & rebounding drills	Sprints	Passing, shooting, & rebounding drills	Sprints
	Offensive or defensive practice		Offensive or defensive practice	
	Endurance running		Endurance running	

The desired conditioning level should be attained by the time competitive play begins, and practices may focus more on skill and teamwork. Drills, scrimmages, and games are generally sufficient to maintain conditioning. For both physical and psychological reasons, practices may be less strenuous or eliminated entirely on game days. Lighter practices may consist of random shooting, free throws, and review of game strategies. To provide rest and diversion, no practice should be held at least one day of the week. The team may also be awarded days off after successive games, as in tournaments, or occasionally to ward off staleness.

Weight Training

With the purchase of multistation weight machines, Exergenies, and free weights, many physical education and athletic programs have begun to use weight training for strength conditioning in a variety of sports. Moving heavy resistance through a few isokinetic repetitions (not exceeding ten) is effective for increasing muscular strength (Knauss 1971). Numerous quick movements against light resistance are recommended to increase muscular endurance.

Particularly during the off-season and preseason, the overload principle should be applied. This may be accomplished by adding weight (resistance) when the player can exceed the maximum number of repetitions established for a particular weight. For example, if a player can consistently press 100 lb for more than ten consecutive repetitions, weight is added to reduce the maximum number of repetitions the player can perform. The muscles are taxed further in attempting to meet the increased work load. To individualize the program, an accurate chart monitoring the progress of each exerciser must be maintained. As an individual exceeds previous personal limits, performance records are invaluable in determining appropriate weight increases.

The following exercises are applicable to a circuit weight training program using free weights and weight machines. Exercises are grouped according to the two major areas of emphasis for strength development in basketball—arms and shoulders, and legs.

Arm Strength Developers

The following exercises contribute to successful shooting, dribbling, and passing:

1. Clean and press

   - Standing with knees flexed, grasp the barbell with an overhand grip and pull weight to the chest.
   - Push upward to an overhead, locked-arm position, using legs to assist in the upward raise.

2. Barbell curl

   - Standing with knees flexed, grasp the barbell with an underhand grip and raise to an erect position with the weight at thigh level.
   - With elbows at sides, flex arms to raise the barbell to the chest.

3. Weight windup

   - Attach a string supporting a 5-lb weight to the center of a broom.
   - Using an overhand grip, rotate the handle to wind the string around it until the weight is raised to the top.
   - Repeat at least three times.

4. Bench press

   - Lie on back on a bench or the floor.
   - Using an overhand grip with the barbell close to the chest, push the weight upward with ten quick repetitions.

- Inhale while bringing the bar to the chest. On completion of each repetition, exhale while elbows are locked.

5.   Side lifts

- With palms facing inward, hold dumbbells at the sides of the body.
- With arms straight, lift dumbbells directly outward and upward until fully overhead.

6.   High pull

- Hold the barbell in front of the thighs, using an overhand grip.
- Raise elbows as high as possible, pulling the weight to the chin.
- Lower the weight and repeat.

7.   Pullovers. (Decrease weight for this exercise.)

- Lie on back, with the barbell placed at arms' length above head.
- Grasp the barbell and pull to a straight-arm position over the chest, keeping elbows close to the body.
- Lower to starting position.
- Inhale on pullover; exhale on lowering.

Leg Strength Developers

The following exercises contribute to successful jumping, rebounding, and shooting:

1.   Calf raise

- Stand with the barbell resting on back of the shoulders.
- Rise on the balls of the feet and return to starting position. (A block of wood under the balls of the feet increases the range of movement in the lower leg muscles.)

2.   Leg presses

- Using a weight machine, sit and rapidly perform ten leg presses to full extension.
- Repeat.

3.   Leg curls

- Lie face down on a table, with the knees extending beyond the table and weights at the back of the ankles.
- Flex the knees, bringing weights toward the buttocks.

4.   Squats

- Stand and grasp the barbell as a partner places it across the shoulders.
- Keeping the back straight, lower to a half squat and rise.
- Repeat ten times.
- An alternative method is to straddle an 18-in. bench with the barbell across the shoulders. Squat until the buttocks touch the bench, keeping the heels on the floor and the back straight.

The weight training session is usually conducted for 45 min to 1 hr. Players should be tested and retested periodically throughout the conditioning program to determine their maximum capabilities.

For off-season and preseason workouts, the player may follow this program:

1. One set of ten repetitions at 50 percent of the maximum weight.
2. Another set of five repetitions at 75 percent of the maximum weight.
3. A third set of three repetitions at 90 percent of the maximum weight.

During the season, the player should maintain strength by performing three sets of ten repetitions at 50 percent of the maximum weight every other day. For best results, no more than 2 min should be allowed between sets.

PROJECTS FOR PROSPECTIVE TEACHERS

1. Design a 10-12-min circuit training warm-up program for a basketball class. Diagram the floor plan, illustrating the various stations and rotation pattern.
2. Compose a series of beginning level skill drills that also promote cardiorespiratory endurance.
3. Devise a basic weight training program designed to improve upper body and leg strength for high school students. Administer the program to yourself three times a week for six weeks, and chart your progress.
4. Observe and compare the conditioning programs of two varsity basketball teams. Determine which components of fitness are developed and to what extent.

References

Barnes, M. *Women's Basketball.* Boston: Allyn and Bacon, 1973.
Knauss, D. "In-season Weight Training Program for Basketball." *Athletic Journal* 52(1971):31.
Moore, B., and White, J. *Basketball: Theory and Practice.* Dubuque, Ia.: William C. Brown Co., 1980.
Ortwerth, J. "Conditioning for Basketball." *Athletic Journal* 53(1972):30.

5

Class Organization

GROUPING FOR PRACTICE

Accommodating students of various levels of skill within the same class is a common problem confronting basketball instructors. Classifying and grouping the students is one way of coping with this range of levels. Players may be grouped according to several factors, including skill (determined by observation of performance and simple skill tests), age, sex, height, and experience. Classifying skill and experience can be particularly effective in providing a safe, enjoyable coeducational setting.

Homogeneous Grouping

When students are homogeneously grouped, the instructor's expectations and teaching techniques may vary from group to group. Expectations should be reasonable for the majority of the students within a classification. Gearing instruction to the similar needs and abilities of all group members enhances learning. The individual is evaluated according to success in meeting expectations established for the group. In the nonthreatening environment that results, students can be challenged, morale improved, and competition regulated.

A departmental team teaching approach can alleviate some of the difficulties associated with instructing varied groupings. Specific techniques will be discussed later in this chapter. If team teaching is not feasible, the instructor can place all class members in homogeneous practice groups where they perform the same activities; the instructor has greater expectations of the more skilled players.

Heterogeneous Grouping

In heterogeneous grouping, each practice group includes an equal distribution of students from each skill, age, height, and experience classification. This composition encourages peer instruction and social interaction. Highly skilled players may be given opportunities for leadership, either by providing examples or through being assigned designated roles within each group. Using homogeneous grouping for instruction and heterogeneous grouping for competition can be an effective option for small classes. This arrangement offers a larger number of teams for tournament play and greater opportunities for the development of interpersonal relationships. By instilling a team concept, the instructor guards against skilled individuals dominating play. Class members should be encouraged to involve all teammates in play and to show recognition of their peers' contributions to the team effort.

TEAM TEACHING

Team teaching offers numerous advantages for instruction in basketball. Allowing teachers to work on activities of their choice and at their level of competence insures adequate instruction for the students. Cooperative planning enables teachers to capitalize on shared knowledge and ideas.

When homogeneous grouping is desired, classes of students scheduled for the same period can be combined and grouped according to some classification. Each teacher or paraprofessional can supervise a different classification. When several classes participate simultaneously in the same activity, full use of indoor and outdoor facilities may be necessary to accommodate the student load. For elective programs, classes can be offered in beginning and advanced basketball. Students opt for the level that best suits their skill and experience. Staffing for the various classes is based on each instructor's level of expertise.

For large or combined heterogeneously grouped classes, a competent instructor can introduce skills and activities to the groups en masse. Following the demonstration, students move into smaller practice groups with assigned instructors, paraprofessionals, or student leaders. The flexibility provided by different-sized groups for instruction and practice may benefit students by offering the possibility of more effective individualized instruction.

INSTRUCTIONAL PROCEDURES

Class Routines

To make the best use of class time, routine class procedures must be handled efficiently. Class should begin on time, with students in designated areas ready for participation. Roll and dress check should take no longer than 3 min, using an expedient method (squad, count off, line-up on numbers, or roll check during warm-up exercises). Instructions should be succinct, so that students may begin active participation as soon as possible.

Teaching Skills

When demonstrating and explaining new skills, the instructor should be visible to the entire seated group. For outdoor demonstrations, the class should be positioned so neither the students nor the instructor must look directly into the sun.

Use of Drills

Once skill techniques have been presented, drills provide opportunities for practice and review. Drills should be selected for their applicability to game situations, and should be easy to understand—the fundamental, not the drill, is the focal point. To accomplish best the specific objective of each drill, students must first understand the purpose and importance of the drill. The instructor must emphasize proper execution, or the students may become accustomed to improper techniques.

In planning a unit, the instructor should include several different activities that drill the same fundamentals; this provides new challenges for the students. To prevent monotony, drills and practice activities should progress in complexity and difficulty. Demanding drills should be followed by less complicated or strenuous ones. In the early part of the season, each lesson should include at least one new drill or activity as well as some repeated drills. Generally, drills should run no longer than 10 min each, depending on the group's interest and capacity for learning. The rule of thumb to follow is to terminate an activity when the interest of the participants peaks.

Teaching Rules

Rules may be taught in conjunction with the appropriate skills or game situations. Demonstrations and opportunities for questions should accompany interpretations of rules. The instructor should take advantage of opportunities to reiterate rules when appropriate situations arise in practice or play.

Teaching Team Play

Once students have mastered basic skills, simple patterns should be used to introduce team strategy and to promote understanding of the role of each player. Although each student should be familiar with all the positions on a team, students quickly recognize their particular suitability for one or two of these. Once students have chosen their positions, they should be given opportunities to develop specific competencies.

When offensive techniques and patterns are initially taught, no defenders should be used. Defenders should be added gradually as the players on offense gain skill and confidence. Basic defensive player-to-player techniques that may apply to all defenses should be taught first. Once the beginners have learned these techniques, zone defenses may be introduced.

Group Size

For the practice of individual skills and basic team tactics, group size depends on the available equipment and facilities and the minimum or maximum number of participants appropriate for the activity. Generally, the fewer the group members, the more practice each participant receives. Small practice groups may also lessen discipline problems and motivate students by creating a more active learning environment. Lulls in activity and lengthy periods of observation often lead to waning interest and vulnerability to distraction.

Although individual work may be advantageous for developing certain skills, team tactics and lead-up activities require larger practice groups to be effective. Groups of even numbers provide flexibility: they can be broken down for partner (one-on-one) or dual (two-on-two) drill work, and reassembled for full group participation.

Ideally, each student or pair of students should have access to a ball for partner drill work. When the supply of basketballs is limited, volleyballs and playground balls may be used for most learning activities. Students using these supplementary balls should be permitted to exchange them periodically for regulation basketballs.

Formations

With larger classes, good organization is necessary to keep all members active. For best use of floor space and equipment, a variety of player formations may be used in skill practice. Fewer balls are required for drills using line formations than for less regimented, nonline organizations such as individual or partner drills. Applicable formations include:

Shuttle Lines (Figure 5.1)

Shuttle lines can be used for passing, receiving, dribbling, and guarding drills. The first player in line A passes or dribbles to the first player in line B, and runs to the end of line B as shown in the

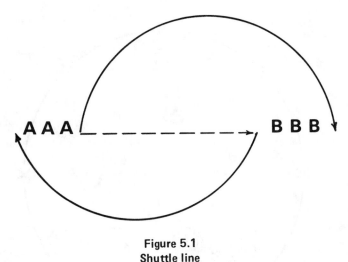

Figure 5.1
Shuttle line

diagram. The first player in line B then passes or dribbles to the next person in line A and runs to the end of line A. For defensive practice, player B (guarding line) attempts to guard player A (dribbling line) while dribbling toward line B. The second player in line A is guarded by the second player in line B, and the one-on-one process continues.

Circle Formation (Figure 5.2)

Circle formation is a useful way to organize passing and receiving drills. Players form a circle and may pass to anyone in the circle except the adjacent players.

Zigzag Formation (Figure 5.3)

Passing and receiving drills can be executed using a zigzag formation. Lines A and B face each other. The first player in line A (A_1) passes to the first player in line B (B_1). Player B_1 then passes the ball to A_2, and players continue diagonally, passing up and down the lines.

Free Throw Formation (Figure 5.4)

The free throw formation can be used for free throw rebounding practice. Six players line up in lane spaces surrounding the free throw lane. One player attempts five free throws from the line as other players attempt to rebound the ball and pass it back to the shooter. Players rotate clockwise after each series of five shots.

Lay-up Formation (Figure 5.5)

The lay-up formation is appropriate for practicing lay-up, set, and jump shooting, as well as rebounding. Divide the team into two lines on opposite sides of the free throw restraining circle. Players are positioned behind the free throw line extended. The first player in the shooting line (S_1) dribbles in, shoots a right-handed lay-up, and moves to the end of the rebounding line. The first rebounder (R_1) grasps the ball; passes to S_2, cutting toward the basket; and moves to the end of the

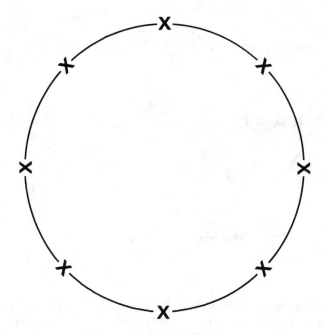

Figure 5.2
Circle formation

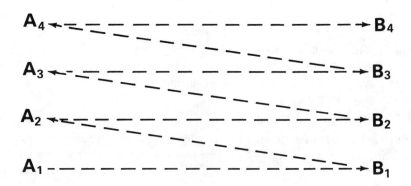

Figure 5.3
Zigzag formation

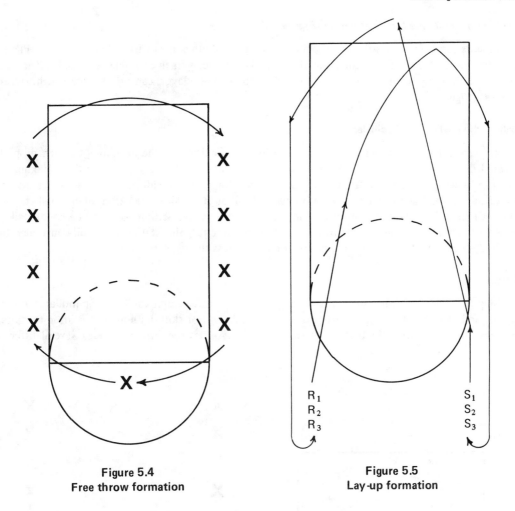

Figure 5.4
Free throw formation

Figure 5.5
Lay-up formation

shooting line. Players continue this pattern until each player has had a set number of attempts. For left-handed lay-ups, the shooting line then switches roles with the rebounding line. Following several of these attempts, the shooting line moves to a position behind the free throw line to execute lay-ups down the center. For set and jump shot practice, the shooter receives a pass from the rebounder and shoots from a spot behind the free throw line extended. Floor areas from which different angled shots may be practiced should be designated.

Single-line Formation (Figure 5.6)

Single-line formation can be used for set or jump shot, dribbling and passing, and lay-up practice. Players line up single file. The first player dribbles and shoots, rebounds the shot, and passes the ball to the next player in line.

Double-Line or Triple-Line Formation (Figure 5.7)

Students can practice passing to a moving player, using double-line or triple-line formation. Players form two or three lines facing the same direction. The first players in each line pass the ball back and forth while moving down the floor and back. With three lines, players can run the figure eight (weave pattern) (Figure 5.8).

Making the Best Use of Facilities

Although a large class can present organizational difficulties for the beginning teacher, properly selected drills can permit 20 to 80 students to be accommodated on the floor at a time. Maximizing use of available facilities permits more practice time for each individual. Group activities may be conducted in small areas that capitalize on available floor and wall space. All available baskets (side and end) should be used for shooting and rebounding practice. Scrimmages may be conducted on each half court, using side baskets to provide four or more teaching stations. For full-court play, the side baskets can provide two or more courts if play is across the regulation court.

Circuit Organization

Using the modified games suggested in Chapter 8, up to three teams can be accommodated at each basket, and sideline players can participate in scrimmages. For skill development, station-to-station organization may provide the best use of available space. Among the different groups, several different

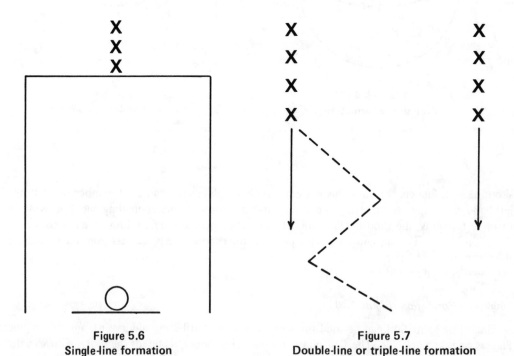

Figure 5.6
Single-line formation

Figure 5.7
Double-line or triple-line formation

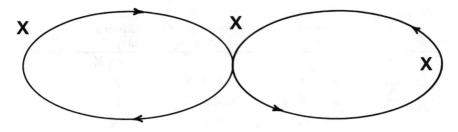

Figure 5.8
Figure eight (weave pattern)

activities may be in progress at the same time. Drills and skill practice for which baskets are unnecessary can be conducted at stations outside the courts, including wall areas. Teams rotate from on-court to off-court drill stations. For the practice of defensive and offensive patterns or nonshooting skills, extra "keyholes" can be taped on the floor outside the court or at midcourt.

A sample circuit organization designed for a large class with 12 practice groups, one teacher, and a facility with six baskets is shown in Figure 5.9.

COEDUCATIONAL PLAY

Under most circumstances, males and females can play together without rules that diminish the competitive opportunities for either sex. Teams should be composed of comparable numbers of male and female players to help regulate competition. When more members are on a team than may be on the court at one time, instructions must be given to assure equal playing time for all participants.

Occasionally, rule modifications may be necessary to encourage total participation and diminish domination of the game by one sex. A few such modifications include:

- Male and female team members play in alternate quarters.
- When the teams on the floor are coeducational, only player-to-player defense may be used, with males guarding males and females guarding females.
- Baskets scored by females count more points than those scored by male players (e.g., field goals, 3 points; free throws, 2 points).
- No more than three male players may represent a team on the floor at any one time.

Other adaptations appear in the two modified games described below.

Corecreational Basketball

1. Divide the class into two teams, A and B, with an equal number of males and females on each team. Players line up on one sideline in the following order: three males from team A, two females from team B, two males from team A, three females from team B, and so forth. On the other sideline, the opposite setup is designated, with three males from team B, two females from team A, and so on, so that opponents of like sex are directly across the floor from each other.

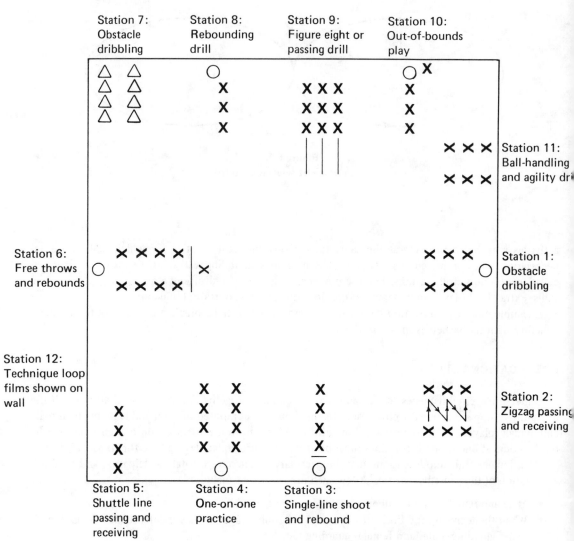

Figure 5.9
Class organization

2. Each team is assigned a basket. To start the game, the first five players from each team take the floor and play for a predetermined 2–5-min period.
3. The remaining players, who are scattered along the sidelines, may receive passes or prevent balls from going out of bounds.
4. Player-to-player defense may be required, with males guarding males, and females guarding females.
5. Regulation rules regarding violations and fouls apply.

Coed Team Basketball

1. Teams are made up of three female and three male players.
2. Male players from both teams play in one half of the court, and female players play in the other half.
3. Each quarter the offensive play alternates between the team's male and female players. The team's three defensive players for that quarter pass the ball across the center line to their offensive counterparts.
4. The game begins with a jump ball between two females or two males.
5. A 10-sec backcourt ruling is enforced.
6. In bonus situations, fouls committed against the defensive team in backcourt are penalized by free throws taken by a designated shooter in the team's offensive court.

BASKETBALL FOR STUDENTS WITH HANDICAPS

With the passage of Public Law 94-142, physical educators are more aware of the need for equal opportunity programs for students with handicaps. With varying degrees of adaptation, the game of basketball is an excellent activity for the mainstreamed or adapted physical education student.

Basketball for Students With Visual Handicaps

Adaptations in equipment and facilities for students who are partially blind include:

- Using larger, softer, more colorful balls
- Placing rattlers or bells inside the balls (see adapted equipment catalogs)
- Lowering goals or using larger goals
- Shortening the distance for free throws
- Using wider line markings

Wheelchair Basketball

Wheelchair basketball is an activity that has recently experienced tremendous growth in recreational and educational programs, including interscholastic sport programs for students with handicaps. To promote safety and better game play, the National Wheelchair Basketball Association has endorsed the following rule adaptations (NWBA 1979):

1. A legal dribble consists of no more than two pushes on the wheels (a) followed by one or more dribbles of the basketball, after which the wheels may be pushed again, or (b) while simultaneously bouncing the ball.
2. On free throws and throw-ins, the large wheels must be behind the line.
3. A legal pivot occurs when a player who is holding the ball turns the chair to the right or left without advancing.
4. An offensive player may not remain longer than 5 sec in the free throw lane while the player's team is in possession of the ball. The rule does not apply when the ball is dead or in flight on a goal attempt, or when a player dribbles in and pivots for a goal.
5. A team loses possession when a player falls out of the chair to gain or maintain possession of the ball.
6. A player cannot touch an opponent or the opponent's chair with the hand.

7. The penalty for a backcourt foul committed by a defensive player is two free throws awarded to the offended player.
8. Each player is classified by degree of motor loss and assigned a number value appropriate to the level of disability. In determining team composition, these values are totaled and a team may not exceed a designated number on the floor at one time.

SAFETY

The instructor is responsible for providing students with the safest possible environment for participation. Although the vigorous nature of basketball creates certain inherent risks, these may be kept to a minimum through good organization and planning. The following precautions can reduce or eliminate accidents or injury to class members:

1. The court area should be clean and clearly marked, with 6 ft of unobstructed space outside the boundary line.
2. Mats should be hung on walls and around permanent objects that are located behind each basket and within 6 ft of the court.
3. Basketballs and other equipment not in use should be removed from the playing area.
4. Players should wear thick socks and basketball shoes with good cushion and traction. All jewelry must be removed.
5. Participants who wear eyeglasses should use guards over them.
6. Proper conditioning, warm-up, and skill execution should be taught.
7. Student leaders may be trained and used as officials to control the game. Apart from student leaders, varsity players in the class or the instructor are the most appropriate officials.
8. Rough play and undesirable conduct must not be allowed.
9. When numerous players are on the court at one time, their movements should be parallel to prevent collisions.
10. All injuries should be reported to the instructor immediately. After attending to the injury, the instructor should file a written account.
11. The instructor should determine class policies, taking into account student suggestions. The policies should be explained to all members and enforced.

TEACHING AIDS

When incorporated into the daily lesson plan, various teaching aids help provide effective motivation and instruction. These include:

- Films, loop films, or video tapes of students in action
- Portable chalkboards or magnetic clipboards for presentations of offensive and defensive play
- Targets on the wall for passing practice
- Cardboard footprints on the floor to indicate footwork
- Tape on the floor to indicate movement patterns
- Demonstrations by local teams
- Field trips to college or professional games
- Music to accompany drill work and warm-ups

STUDENT LEADERSHIP

Student leadership can be an invaluable source of assistance to the teacher or coach; it also affords participants opportunities for peer recognition and the development of leadership qualities. Students can be selected and trained to assist in classes through an organized leadership program or club in the department. After a training period in which they become familiar with rules, officiating, demonstration techniques, and leadership responsibilities, the leaders are assigned to the instructors for designated periods.

In situations in which student leadership programs are nonexistent, the instructor may appoint or the group may elect class leaders. Students who are to act as captains or group leaders must be given guidance regarding their responsibilities and attitude. Evaluating leaders on their proficiency in performing their tasks helps reinforce their sense of the importance of their roles.

Student leaders whom the instructor appoints are generally the most competent in performing their tasks. When leaders are elected, however, peer support is greater. To offer all or most of the students an opportunity, leaders may be changed for each activity unit. This also lessens possible accusations of favoritism in cases in which the instructor chooses the leaders. A limitation of electing leaders is that the students who are chosen may be popular but not qualified as leaders. Elected or appointed leaders who are negligent in handling their responsibilities should be replaced immediately.

The following is a list of responsibilities frequently delegated to student leaders:

- Handling routine class details (roll call, checking facilities and equipment for safety, leading opening exercises)
- Accounting for equipment
- Conducting drill work in practice groups and acting as a squad leader
- Officiating, scoring, or keeping statistics
- Administering skill tests
- Demonstrating skills
- Assisting in program planning

PROJECTS FOR PROSPECTIVE TEACHERS

1. Diagram a floor plan of eight teaching stations for 40 students on one basketball court.
2. Research two methods of arriving at teams of comparable ability for tournament play.
3. Conduct a coeducational basketball game or tournament as an intramural event at a high school.

Reference

National Wheelchair Basketball Association. *Official Rules and Case Book.* Lexington, Ky.: NWBA, 1979.

6

Teaching
Beginning Skills

Before participating in the game of basketball, students should attain some degree of skill in the fundamentals. All players must be able to catch, pass, shoot, and dribble the ball; rebound; pivot; and play a little defense. A player's proficiency in these fundamentals determines the level of play to which he or she may progress.

Each of the player positions—guard, forward, and center—calls for a variety of skills with varying degrees of refinement. For example, certain positions may require greater skill in ball handling, while others demand strong rebounding abilities. Size often influences a player's suitability for a position and the appropriate skills to be emphasized.

FOOTWORK

A certain knowledge of fundamental footwork is essential to anyone wishing to become a basketball player. A player must know how to start and stop, change direction quickly, and pivot.

Starts

The ability to start quickly from a standing position is vital to becoming a good basketball player.

Performance Description

1. Lean in the direction of the intended run.
2. Dig the feet into the floor as if running on snow or soft sand.
3. Take short, choppy steps on the start, and lengthen the stride as speed increases.
4. Use arms in a pumping motion, both for balance and to help acceleration.

Common Errors

1. Attempting to start from a straight-up position
2. Attempting to start with weight on heels
3. First step too long

Stops

Stopping quickly, without taking additional steps, is just as important as starting quickly. Players must learn to stop properly to avoid traveling violations and charging fouls. The two methods of stopping are the jump stop and the stride stop.

Jump Stop

Performance Description

1. While running, make a short jump and land on both feet simultaneously. Keep the feet well spread, and bend the knees to absorb the shock.
2. Drop the hips low.
3. Shift weight to the balls of the feet and the heels.
4. Use hands and arms for balance.

Stride Stop

Performance Description

1. While running, make a short jump and land with a one-two count, one foot in front of the other. Bend the knees to absorb the shock.
2. Drop the hips low.
3. Shift weight to the balls of the feet and the heels.
4. Use hands and arms for balance.

Common Errors

1. Feet too close together on the stop
2. Failure to drop the hips
3. Failure to shift weight as the stop is made

Changing Direction

A quick change of direction often frees an offensive player to receive a pass. Quick change of direction is also necessary to guard an offensive opponent closely.

Performance Description

1. While running, plant the right foot firmly on the court.
2. Drop the left shoulder.
3. Look to the left.
4. Step to the left with the left foot, using the arms and hands for balance.
5. Reverse the process to change direction to the right.

Pivots

A player holding the ball may step in any direction with one foot as long as the other foot—the pivot foot—keeps its contact point with the floor. After a player has made a jump stop or caught the ball while stationary, either foot may become the pivot foot. Following a dribble or a two-step stop with the ball, only the rear foot may become the pivot foot.

The pivot is used primarily to allow the player in possession of the ball to protect it from the defensive opponent. Some players use it in an offensive attack. The beginning player should learn both the rear pivot and the front pivot.

Rear Pivot

Performance Description

1. While running, come to a jump stop with the body crouched and the right foot slightly forward or the feet parallel.
2. Keep the ball of the left foot on the floor.
3. Drop the right shoulder and the right hip.
4. Push backward with the right foot and swing the right elbow to the rear.
5. Come to a stop, facing the opposite direction.
6. For a rear pivot to the left, reverse the procedure.

Front Pivot

Performance Description

1. While running, come to a jump stop with the body crouched and the left foot slightly forward or the feet parallel.
2. Keep the ball of the left foot on the floor.
3. Drop the left shoulder.
4. Push forward with the right foot and swing the right leg forward and around.
5. Come to a stop, facing the opposite direction.
6. Reverse the procedure for a right front pivot.

Common Errors

1. Failure to keep the pivot foot in contact with the floor
2. Dragging the pivot foot, which results in a traveling violation
3. Pivoting in the wrong direction

Teaching Tips

1. Insist that the students think about the pivot. Students often try to hurry through it, and pivot in the wrong direction.
2. Pivots should be done in a crouched position; if the player is in possession of the ball, it should be protected with the body and arms.

Drills

Start, Stop, and Pivot Drill

Divide the class into four lines. The first player in each line starts on command, runs to a designated spot, comes to a jump stop, executes a rear pivot, starts, and runs back to the starting point, coming to a stride stop. After each player has a turn, repeat the drill using the front pivot. Dribbling may also be incorporated into this drill.

Change of Direction Drill

Each player has a partner. Starting at midcourt, one player is on defense while the other makes several changes of direction, trying to get free for a pass and a lay-up shot. When the offensive player gets free, the instructor under the basket passes the ball. The players exchange places and repeat the drill.

HANDLING THE BALL

Before any of the basic skills can be taught, the player must know how to hold and handle the ball properly.

Performance Description

1. Lay the basketball on the floor.
2. Spread the fingers of both hands as wide as possible without discomfort.
3. Place the fingertips of each hand on the sides of the ball.
4. Pick up the ball with the fingertips, and bring the thumbs behind and toward the middle of the ball (Figure 6.1).

Common Errors

1. Fingers spread too wide
2. Letting the palms of the hands touch the ball

Teaching Tips

1. Constantly remind students to handle the ball using only the fingertips.
2. Encourage students to handle the ball as much as possible.

Drills

Waist Circle Drill

Holding the ball with the fingertips, shift the ball around the waist as rapidly as possible. Alternate directions.

Leg Wrap Drill

Holding the ball with the fingertips, wind it around the legs. Alternate directions. Do a figure eight around the legs.

Walking Wrap Drill

Holding the ball with the fingertips, wind the ball around the legs while walking the length of the court.

Figure 6.1
Handling the ball

Quick Hands Drill

With the right hand behind the legs and the left hand in front, hold the ball between the legs with the fingertips. Release the ball, quickly reverse the position of the hands, and catch the ball with the fingertips before it falls to the floor. Repeat rapidly.

CATCHING

Two of the most important factors in catching the basketball are (1) keeping your eye on the ball until it is in your hands and (2) concentrating on catching the ball. Most fumbles are caused by a player's failure to attend to one of these rules.

Performance Description

1. Spread the fingers and point them in a relaxed position either up or down, depending on the height of the pass.

2. Reach toward the pass.
3. Watch the ball move into your hands. Concentrate on catching the ball.
4. As the ball makes contact with the fingertips, flex the elbows and give with the hands and arms to absorb the force of the ball.
5. Draw the arms back to a passing position.

Common Errors

1. Taking the eyes off the ball, resulting in a fumble or missed catch
2. Catching the ball with the palms
3. Failure to absorb the force of the ball properly when it makes contact, resulting in injured fingers or a fumble

Teaching Tips

1. When the pass is at waist level or above, the thumbs should be pointed inward, and the fingers should be up.
2. When the pass is below the waist, the thumbs should be pointed outward, with the fingers down.

PASSING

Next to shooting, passing is rated as the most important fundamental in basketball. Accuracy and timing in passing are generally the key to successful team play. Since most situations require that passes be aimed between the receiver's chest and waist, beginners should concentrate on mastering passes to that area.

Three passes are considered essential for all players—the chest pass, the bounce pass, and the flip pass.

Chest Pass

The msot common pass in basketball is the chest pass. Generally used for distances of about 20 ft, the chest pass is an accurate way to move the ball quickly.

Performance Description

1. Hold the ball in both hands, with the fingers spread and the thumbs pointing toward each other on the back of the ball (Figure 6.2).
2. Bend the elbows, keeping them comfortably close to the sides of the body.
3. Balance the body on both feet in a stride position.
4. Release the ball with a push of the arms, a straightening of the elbows, and a snap of the wrists. Aim at the teammate's chest.
5. As the ball is released, shift the weight of the body toward the receiver.
6. Follow through with the arms and fingers fully extended toward the receiver and the palms turned outward (Figure 6.3).

Figure 6.2
Chest pass stance

Figure 6.3
Chest pass follow-through

Common Errors

1. Failure to concentrate on hitting the target spot
2. Not giving enough speed to the ball
3. Incomplete follow-through, resulting in weak or misguided passes

Teaching Tips

1. Having the students exaggerate the turning of the palms to the outside after releasing the ball will help them follow through more completely and become more accurate with their passes.
2. Placing the students behind a line and requiring them to step across the line on every pass will also help them develop accuracy.

Bounce Pass

The bounce pass is used to transfer the ball to a closely guarded teammate or when an opponent is in the way. Although it is similar to the chest pass, it is directed to a spot on the floor near the feet of the opponent and under the opponent's outstretched arms so that it will bounce up to the intended receiver.

Performance Description

1. Hold the ball in both hands with the fingers spread and the thumbs pointing toward each other on the back of the ball.
2. Bend the elbows, keeping them comfortably close to the sides of the body.
3. Balance the body on both feet in a stride position.
4. Release the ball with a push of the arms, a straightening of the elbows, and a snap of the wrists. Aim at a spot on the floor so that the ball rebounds to the hip area of a teammate on the side away from the defensive opponent.
5. As the ball is released, step toward the target spot on the floor.
6. Follow through with the arms and fingers fully extended toward the target spot and the palms turned outward.

Common Errors

1. Failure to give enough speed to the ball
2. Failure to hit the proper target spot
3. Failure to step toward the intended target on release
4. Incomplete follow-through

Flip Pass

The flip pass is used for a close exchange of the ball, as in a hand-off from a high post player to a cutter. The movement of the ball is mostly upward. The flip pass should be used only for short passes.

Performance Description

1. Stand with the weight balanced on both feet.
2. Place the passing hand directly under the ball.
3. With a flip of the wrist, propel the ball to a stationary receiver, aiming for the waist area.
4. Using the same procedure, flip the ball to a receiver who is moving toward the basket.

Common Errors

1. Flipping the ball too hard
2. Flipping the ball too high
3. Failure to pass the ball in front of a moving receiver

Drills

Many of the drills frequently used for passing and catching may be used with any of the basic passes. The following drills are adaptable to each of the fundamental passes.

Circle Drill (Figure 6.4)

Divide the class into groups of six or seven. In each group, have all players except one form a circle about 15 ft in diameter. Place one player in the middle of the circle. Using any type of pass, the

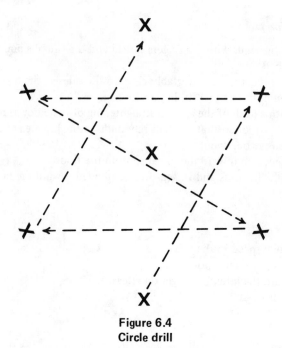

Figure 6.4
Circle drill

players forming the circle try to prevent the player in the middle from touching the ball. Once a pass is touched, the passer replaces the middle player. No player may pass the ball to an adjacent player.

Two-Ball Drill

One player stands facing five or six other players. The one player has a ball, and one of the end players in the line has a ball. The one player passes the ball to the second player in line while receiving a pass from the adjacent player. Each player tries to time the pass with that of the single player, who tries to pass to each player in turn. The single player is given two misses. Then another player goes out in front.

DRIBBLING

All players occasionally find themselves in a situation in which dribbling the ball is necessary to elude a defensive opponent or to move the ball. Because many teachers and coaches discourage excessive dribbling, some players are not given the opportunity to develop and refine this skill.

Performance Description

1.   Balance the weight on the toes with the body crouched and the knees bent to a quarter bend.
2.   The arm of the dribbling hand should have the elbow positioned low, with the forearm parallel to the floor. The nondribbling hand should be held about waist high and comfortably to that side of the body. Keep the body between the ball and the defensive opponent (Figure 6.5).

Figure 6.5
Dribbling stance

3. With the fingers comfortably spread, push the ball to the floor slightly in front of and to the side of the body, snapping the wrist and making a slight downward motion with the forearm.
4. As the ball rebounds from the floor, control it with the fingertips, giving with the wrist and forearm, and push it down again. Bounce the ball to about hip height.
5. Keep the head up. Do not look at the ball while dribbling.
6. Change hands and dribble with the other hand.

Common Errors

1. Touching the ball with the palms while dribbling
2. Dribbling too high, thereby losing control
3. Looking at the ball while dribbling rather than looking ahead

Teaching Tips

1. In the beginning, students should not attempt to dribble with great speed. They should concentrate on developing a feel for the ball and fingertip control.
2. After mastering the dribble at slow speed, students should work on developing control at full speed.

Drills

Dribble Relay

Divide the class into teams of four or five. The first person on each team dribbles the length of the court with the right hand, and returns dribbling with the left hand. Each player takes a turn, and the first team finished is the winner.

Blindfold Dribble

Divide the class into pairs. Blindfold one stationary player who dribbles the ball, changing hands frequently. The blindfolded player's partner is alert to the safety of the dribbler and retrieves the ball if it is lost. Partners exchange roles every 90 sec.

Dribble Derby

Place two players, each with a ball, in each of the jump circles on the court. While dribbling, each player tries to knock away the opponent's ball. Change players every 30 sec. To motivate students, an elimination contest may be run using this drill.

SHOOTING

Many teachers and coaches consider shooting to be the most important fundamental in basketball. Regardless of how well a team may dribble, pass, and rebound, without good shooting it is not likely to win. A famous coach once said, "God taught the boy to shoot and I took the credit." Such a statement supports the belief that great shooters are born with a good touch. While this may or may not be true, most good shooters combine sound fundamental techniques with long hours of practice.

Nothing substitutes for long hours of practice. Remember that practice does not make perfect— perfect practice makes perfect. Players should be encouraged to view each practice attempt as if it were the winning shot in a game. If practice is taken casually, bad habits may be formed.

Beginning players must be able to execute three basic shots properly—the lay-up, the free throw, and the jump shot.

Lay-up Shot

The lay-up, or "crip," shot is the first fundamental shot the player should learn. A player takes a lay-up at the end of a drive or after receiving a pass while cutting for the basket.

Performance Description

1. For a right-handed lay-up, stand on the right side of the basket facing the backboard at an angle of about 45 degrees.
2. Place the weight on the left foot, and hold the ball in the right hand.
3. Look at a spot on the backboard about 12–15 in. above the right side of the rim, reach as high as possible with the right hand, and raise the body up onto the left foot.
4. Push the ball against the target spot on the backboard as softly as possible.
5. Adjust the target spot on the backboard until the ball drops through the net each time.
6. Take one step back and place the weight on the right foot.
7. Step forward onto the left foot and repeat the shooting process.
8. Practice this footwork until it is comfortable.
9. Hold the ball in both hands. On the approach, move it to the right hand when starting the ascent from the left foot. Complete the shot.
10. Move back another step with the weight on the left foot and hold the ball in both hands. Step out on the right foot, and then leap upward off the left foot and complete the shot as before (Figure 6.6).

Figure 6.6
Lay-up shot

11.   Move out onto the court and dribble in to shoot the lay-up shot.
12.   After receiving a pass near the basket, take the lay-up shot without dribbling first.

Common Errors

1.   Jumping off the wrong foot
2.   Failure to look at the target spot on the backboard before releasing the ball
3.   Forcefully caroming the ball off the backboard rather than laying it up softly
4.   Failure to place the ball high enough on the backboard

Teaching Tips

1.   Form should precede speed. Once the shot has been properly executed, emphasize 100 percent accuracy on lay-ups in practice.
2.   Stress the point that the leap is not a broad jump and that the emphasis should be on getting as high as possible.
3.   When making this shot, the student should reach upward toward the target spot as far as possible. The top right-hand corner of the rectangle painted on fiberglass backboards provides an excellent target for right-side lay-ups.

4. To teach the lay-up shot with the left hand, reverse the footwork and shift the target spot to the left. If they are required to go through these steps each day, most students can learn to use the nondominant hand within a few days.
5. Lay-up drills should be a regular part of each day's warm-up process. When lay-up drills are used as warm-up exercises, have students start off slowly and increase speed gradually.

Drills

Two-Line Drill

Divide the class into two lines. Put one line on each side of the court at the center line. Have members of one line dribble in and shoot a right-handed lay-up, while those in the other line rebound and pass the ball out to the next player in the shooting line. Shooter and rebounder return to the end of the opposite line. After each player has had three shots, reverse roles for each line.

Lay-up Relay

Divide the class into two equal squads, and station them at opposite ends of the court behind the end line. Have each player dribble the length of the court with the right hand, shoot a right-handed lay-up, retrieve the ball, return while dribbling with the left hand, and shoot a left-handed lay-up. All shots must go into the basket.

Free Throw (Push Shot)

A basic shot that all players must be able to make successfully is the free throw. An unpublished study by one of the coauthors (Reynolds) indicates that over 70 percent of all high school and college level basketball games are won or lost at the free throw line. In an average high school or college game, free throws account for approximately 20 percent of the total points scored.

Although many different types of shots are used for making the free throw, the general belief is that only one basic shot should be taught to beginning players—the push shot. The push shot also may be used for field goal shooting when the player cannot obtain a suitable jump shot.

Performance Description (Right-handed)

1. Stand with the right foot about 1 in. behind the free throw line.
2. Place the left foot so that the toes are about even with the instep of the right foot. The feet should be about shoulder width apart.
3. The body should be balanced, although most of the weight should be on the front foot.
4. Bend the knees slightly.
5. Place the left hand underneath the ball for balance; place the right hand behind the ball, with the index finger in the center of the ball and the wrist cocked.
6. Using the index finger as a guide, look just over the ball for the top of the front edge of the rim.
7. Keep the elbow of the shooting arm under the ball and in a straight line between the shoulder and the basket (Figure 6.7).
8. Put the ball in motion by straightening the knees, moving the elbow upward, and pushing forward with the forearm and wrist. These movements should occur simultaneously (Figure 6.8).
9. As the ball leaves the index finger, reach toward the basket and snap the wrist to complete the follow-through (Figure 6.9).

Figure 6.7
Free throw (push shot) stance

Figure 6.8
Free throw (push shot) ball release

Figure 6.9
Free throw (push shot) follow-through

Common Errors

1. Failure to keep the body balanced
2. Failure to concentrate on the target spot
3. Failure to project the ball with sufficient arc
4. Bringing the hand across the body after the shot

Teaching Tips

1. Mental practice before each shot helps many players.
2. The shooter must learn to relax at the free throw line. Have the players bounce the ball two or three times and take a deep breath before shooting.
3. On the follow-through, require that the shooter turn the palm of the shooting hand to the outside. This insures that the ball comes off the index finger last and helps develop the soft touch.

Drills

Freeze-out Drill

Players line up single file at the free throw line. The first player attempts a shot; if successful, the second player must do likewise or be "frozen out" and sit down. If the first player misses, the next player in line is not disqualified for a miss. If the second player's shot is successful, the third player must make the shot or be frozen out. Continue the procedure; the last player remaining is the winner.

Risk It Drill

Arrange a series of seven spots at a distance of about 15 ft from the basket. The first player in line shoots from the number 1 spot. If the shot is made, the shooter continues to the number 2 spot and shoots again. After each successful shot, the shooter progresses to the next spot. If the shot is missed at any spot other than number 1, the shooter may go to the back of the line and wait another turn to continue from that spot, or the shooter may opt to risk another shot. If the risk shot is made, the shooter continues as before. If the risk shot is missed, the shooter must await another turn and start over at the number 1 spot. First player to complete the circuit is the winner.

Jump Shot

The jump shot has become the most popular and effective shot in basketball. The jump shot is popular because it is difficult to defend against.

Performance Description

1. Face the basket with the shoulders square. Hold the ball in both hands (Figure 6.10).
2. Keep the body balanced on both feet.
3. From a quarter knee bend, push straight upward with both legs (Figure 6.11).
4. As the body goes up, turn the ball with the left hand so that the left hand is underneath the ball for balance.
5. Place the right hand behind the ball, with the index finger at the center line of the ball and the wrist cocked.

6. Bring the ball to a position just above and in front of the head. Keep the elbow of the shooting arm under the ball and in a straight line between the shoulder and the basket.
7. Sight just under the ball for the top of the nearest edge of the rim.
8. Release the ball with a quick extension of the elbow and a flick of the wrist and fingers of the shooting hand.
9. Snap the wrist completely forward for a good follow-through (Figure 6.12).
10. While dribbling, take a couple of steps in any direction and repeat the above procedure.

Common Errors

1. Failure to maintain body balance throughout the shot
2. Failure to concentrate on hitting the target spot
3. Jumping forward rather than straight up
4. Releasing the ball while descending rather than at the peak of the jump
5. Bringing the shooting hand across the body on the follow-through

Figure 6.10
Jump shot stance

Figure 6.11
Jump shot preparation

Figure 6.12
Jump shot follow-through

Teaching Tips

1. Most students are eager to learn the jump shot from about 15–18 ft. Insist that the shooter start at 8 ft; once proficient at that distance, the shooter can move to 10 ft. Distance should be increased only after success is achieved at close range.
2. Body balance is easier to maintain when the shooter lands on the take-off spot. Constantly remind the students to jump straight up and come straight down. This also eliminates the possibility of charging into a defensive opponent during the shot.
3. Insist that the shooter turn the palm of the shooting hand to the outside on the follow-through. This insures that the ball comes off the index finger last.

Drill

Jump Shot Drill

Set up one or more chairs at various spots around the basket. The shooter dribbles up to the chair, stops, jumps, and shoots. This drill helps the shooter learn to land on the take-off spot. To make the drill more like a game, replace the chair with another player.

REBOUNDING

Rebounding missed shots is one of the most important aspects of basketball. Since even the best teams miss approximately 50 percent of their attempted shots, the team that is able to grab the most rebounds during a game is usually the winner.

One misconception among beginning players is that being tall is necessary to take a rebound. Good shorter players, however, often get more than their share of the defensive and offensive rebounds.

Defensive Rebounding

Any time the opponent takes a shot, the defensive player must be ready to rebound immediately. The task of this player is twofold—preventing the opponent from getting the rebound and obtaining the rebound.

Performance Description

1. As the shot goes up, watch the opponent.
2. Execute a rear pivot in the direction the opponent is moving.
3. Make contact with the arms spread slightly back. Put the back toward the opponent.
4. Use the slide step to maintain a position between the opponent and the ball (Figure 6.13).
5. As the ball descends, take a position beneath it. From a quarter knee bend, leap as high as possible, fully extending the body; grab the ball with both hands and come down in a crouch. Widen the stance and spread the arms to use as much room as possible.
6. Use the arms and body to protect the ball.

Figure 6.13
Defensive rebounding

Common Errors

1.   Failure to pivot in the right direction
2.   Failure to make contact with the opponent
3.   Going after the ball too soon
4.   Moving too far under the basket, allowing the ball to rebound over the head
5.   Failure to protect the ball after the rebound

Teaching Tips

1.   Rebounding requires timing and coordination. Use a variety of activities to help students develop these skills.
2.   Show students that a short player can rebound effectively by practicing the proper fundamentals.
3.   Stress that just preventing the opponent from getting the rebound is important.

Offensive Rebounding

Offensive rebounding is one of the most difficult facets of basketball to teach. Once a player has grasped the fundamentals of defensive rebounding, however, offensive rebounding seems to come more easily. With the knowledge that the defensive player's job is to block out, the offensive player must offset the defensive player's inside position advantage.

Performance Description

1.   As the shot goes up, move away from the defensive player. Do not allow the defensive player to make physical contact.
2.   Get the inside position by feinting in one direction and moving in another.
3.   Block out the defensive player as described in defensive rebounding.
4.   Grab the rebound; either put up another shot if in a favorable position or pass off to a teammate.

Common Errors

1.   Reacting too slowly after the shot has been taken
2.   Allowing the defensive player to block out
3.   Failure to rebound aggressively

Teaching Tips

1.   The offensive player must go after the rebound the instant the shot is started. Reaction drills are helpful.
2.   Good fakes and changes of direction are necessary skills for the offensive rebounder.

Drills

Form Drill

Divide the class into four or more groups and have each group form a line at center court. The first player in each line dribbles into the free throw line area and tosses the ball against the backboard.

This player then takes a rebound in good form and passes the ball out to the next player in line. The first player goes to the back of the line. Repeat several times.

Tear-away Drill

Divide the class into four or more groups and have each group form a line at center court. The first player in line dribbles into the free throw line area and tosses the ball against the backboard. This player rebounds the ball, while the second and third players in line attempt to tear the ball out of the first player's hands. The first player goes to the back of the line and the second player becomes the rebounder while the third and fourth players attempt to tear the ball away.

Three-on-Three Drill

Put three players on offense and three players on defense around the free throw line area. The offensive team shoots the ball and tries for the offensive rebound. The defensive team tries to block out and rebound. The defensive players stay on defense until they have gotten the ball five times.

INDIVIDUAL DEFENSE

No one can become a well-rounded player and achieve success in basketball without being able—and willing—to play defense. Defense is both a physical and a mental undertaking. Undoubtedly it is the most physically demanding part of the game. Contrary to the belief of many beginning players, time on defense is not the time to catch one's breath. Trying to rest on defense usually results in a score for the opponent.

Individual defense can be broken down into two categories—guarding the opponent with the ball and guarding the opponent without the ball. In either situation, individual defensive skills are generally the same, and depend on four major factors—stance, footwork, position, and vision.

Stance

Quickness in individual defensive play is necessary to counteract the movement of the offensive player. A proper stance is a must in order to move quickly. Among the best players, the boxer's stance is the most commonly used (Figure 6.14).

Performance Description

1. Spread the feet about shoulder width apart, with the toe of one foot even with the instep of the other.
2. Bend the knees to about a quarter bend and keep the hips down.
3. Place the weight forward on the toes, evenly distributed on both feet.
4. The back should be at a 45-degree angle to the floor.
5. Keep the head up.
6. For quick starts, arms should be kept down initially to lower the center of gravity.
7. When guarding a stationary player, one hand should be over the ball and the other to the side. The forward foot and hand over the ball should correspond. Attempts to steal the ball should be made with upward hand movements.

Figure 6.14
Boxer's stance for individual defense

Common Errors

1. Feet not far enough apart
2. Weight placed on heels
3. Failure to maintain balance
4. Looking at floor

Teaching Tips

1. Demonstrate to the class the elements of a good stance.
2. Show the class how much more quickly one can move from a good stance than from a poor one.

Drill

Breakdown Drill

At the signal "break down" from the instructor, which is given at any time during class, students assume a good defensive stance. Each student holds this position until the instructor checks the stance.

Defensive Footwork

Footwork is an important aspect of defense and is based on the slide step. By taking short, rapid steps, the defensive player can move and change direction quickly.

Performance Description

1. Assume a good defensive stance.
2. Slide the right foot to the right 12–15 in.
3. Slide the left foot into a position near the right foot.
4. Repeat the slide step several times.
5. Do the slide step to the left by reversing the procedure.

Common Errors

1. Failure to keep weight on the toes
2. Failure to stay low
3. Straightening the body while moving
4. Crossing the feet while moving

Drill

Box Drill

Line up the class in an open military formation with about 5-ft intervals between students and rows. Students assume the defensive stance. On a signal from the instructor, the class slide-steps to the right, to the left, forward, and backward. Use sight signals and give the commands in various orders.

Position

Ninety percent of defense has been said to be position—being in the right place at the right time. Regardless of how quick a defensive player is or how correct the stance, if the player is not in the proper floor position, little defense takes place. Generally, the defensive player should remain in a direct line between the opponent and the basket. *Never* let the opponent go straight to the basket. If an offensive player consistently drives in the same direction, the defender should overplay—adjust position with one foot opposite the midline of the opponent and the other foot to the side of the expected drive. An overplay may be appropriate to force an opponent in a predetermined direction or into a well-defended area.

One notable exception occurs when the opponent is near the basket, as in the case of a pivot player. In that situation, the defensive player should take a position beside or between the offensive opponent and the ball to prevent the opponent from getting the ball into a favorable position for scoring.

When guarding an opponent in possession of the ball, the speed of that player determines the defender's strategy. If the opponent is a good shooter, the defender must play close. If the opponent is not a good shooter but is fast, the defender must stay back a couple of steps so that the opponent cannot drive past on a quick move. The arm closest to the sideline is extended out to the side, while the other arm reaches toward the offensive player.

When guarding an opponent without the ball, the defender should drop back a couple of steps toward the basket and turn slightly toward the ball. The defensive stance is maintained with the arm closest to the ball extended outward and the other arm pointing toward the opponent. When the ball is far from the player being guarded, the defender moves closer to the basket. As the ball comes nearer the guarded player, the defender moves toward that player.

Performance Description

1. Positioned between the opponent with the ball and the basket, assume a defensive stance.
2. Move with the opponent, keeping in a direct line between the opponent and the basket. Use the slide step.
3. Once the opponent has dribbled, guard closely, with one hand low and the other over the ball, attempting to force a shooting or passing mistake or turnover.
4. When the opponent passes the ball to a teammate, open the stance toward the ball and drop back two short steps. Be aware of the location of the ball at all times.

Common Errors

1. Relaxing on defense
2. Failure to maintain a good stance
3. Failure to watch the opponent closely
4. Stumbling as a result of an opponent's feint
5. Losing sight of the ball

Teaching Tips

1. Beginning students should be taught to play position defense without using their hands. Requiring them to keep their hands folded behind their back is usually effective.
2. At various times during drills, blow the whistle and have everyone freeze in place. Point out the students in good defensive position and those in poor defensive position.

Drill

Position Drill

Divide the class into teams of five players. Use one team for offense and one for defense. "Set" the offense and have them pass the ball. Have the defensive players change position in relation to the ball. Start slowly and increase the speed at which the ball is moving as the defense learns to adjust. Rotate the teams from offense to defense.

Vision

Good defensive players need to develop the ability to see not only what is in front of them but also what is taking place on either side. When guarding a player with the ball, the defender should watch that player's midsection, as that part of the body is not used in a feint. When guarding a player without the ball, the defender should focus on a spot about midway between the ball and the opponent being guarded. This allows the defender to see both the ball and the opponent.

A good defensive player must be intent on stopping the opponent. The player must study the opponent, making mental notes of the strengths and weaknesses of that player. The defender's task is then to neutralize the strengths and capitalize on the weaknesses.

PROJECTS FOR PROSPECTIVE TEACHERS

1. Diagram and explain at least one drill for each of the following fundamentals: chest pass, bounce pass, dribble, defensive rebounding.
2. Develop a 40-min lesson plan on shooting that includes time for taking roll, warm-up exercises, demonstrations, and evaluation.

7

Teaching Advanced Skills

The basic skills described in Chapter 6 allow the average individual to play basketball for enjoyment and exercise. In addition to refining their grasp of fundamental skills, advanced players should master additional skills that will enable them to achieve a greater degree of success.

ADVANCED PASSING TECHNIQUES

The basic passes described earlier are necessary for all players. Once these passes can be executed comfortably, the player who wishes to advance further is ready to work on additional passing skills such as the one-hand pass, the baseball pass, the hook pass, and the two-hand overhead pass.

One-Hand Pass

The advanced player frequently uses the one-hand pass. This pass allows the offensive player a greater degree of deception than do other passes. It can be either an air pass or a bounce pass. Skilled ball handlers can execute the pass off the dribble without first having to catch the ball in both hands.

Performance Description

1. Place the passing hand behind the basketball, touching the ball with the fingertips only (Figure 7.1).
2. The hand not passing may be under and slightly in front of the ball for support.
3. With a pushing motion toward the receiver, or the target spot for a bounce pass, release the ball with a snap of the wrist.
4. Follow through with an extension of the arm toward the receiver or target spot. For longer passes, shift the weight toward the flight of the ball.

Common Errors

1. Letting the ball rest on the palm of the hand rather than on the fingertips
2. Incomplete follow-through

Figure 7.1
One-hand pass

Teaching Tips

1. When practicing this pass, have the students step in various directions to execute the pass.
2. Students should practice a variety of one-hand passes with each hand. To make the most use of the one-hand pass, the advanced player should be able to execute the pass with either hand.
3. Point out the vulnerable passing areas around the defensive player—near the foot, over the shoulder of the lowered arm, over the head of short players.
4. Have the students practice combining one or more feints with their passes.

Baseball (Overarm) Pass (Figure 7.2)

The baseball pass is a special type of one-hand pass designed for long-distance throwing down the floor. Teams that employ the fast break use it extensively.

Performance Description

1. The right-handed player should point the left shoulder in the direction of the intended flight of the ball. Place the weight on the right foot.
2. With the right hand behind the ball, use the left hand for support and bring the ball to a position behind the right ear. The index finger of the right hand should be in the center of the ball.
3. Bring the hand, arm, and shoulder forward and step with the left foot in the direction of the intended receiver.
4. As the ball nears the release point, extend the arm and snap the wrist, letting the ball come off the index finger. Shift the body weight to the left foot.
5. Follow through by stepping toward the receiver onto the right foot and dropping the arm down.

Figure 7.2
Baseball (overarm) pass

Common Errors

1. Attempting to throw the ball with the palm of the hand rather than the fingertips
2. Releasing the ball off the side of the hand rather than the fingertips, causing the ball to curve in flight
3. Incomplete follow-through

Teaching Tips

1. When practicing this pass, students should start with short passes of about 25 ft; as they learn to execute the pass properly, the distance should be increased gradually to prevent possible arm injuries.
2. Emphasize the importance of executing this pass properly to prevent the ball from curving in flight.
3. This pass is not recommended for the smaller or weaker player.

Hook Pass

Although it is difficult to control, the hook pass is excellent for passing the ball over an opponent after getting a defensive rebound. It can also be used when the passer is moving down the side of the court with a defensive opponent alongside and the intended receiver is near the center of the court. The fast-breaking team uses the hook pass extensively.

Performance Description

1. Place the right hand under the ball and extend the right arm fully away from the body. The left hand may be used to support the ball if necessary.
2. Step onto the left foot, with the left shoulder pointing toward the receiver. Look at the receiver.
3. With a sweeping motion, bring the right hand directly over the head.
4. As the right hand passes over the head, release the ball with a snap of the wrist.
5. Follow through by pointing the index finger toward the receiver.

Common Errors

1. Attempting to pass the ball with the palm of the hand rather than the fingertips
2. Releasing the ball too soon
3. Failure to follow through by snapping the wrist and pointing the fingers at the receiver

Teaching Tips

1. Students should begin by practicing this pass at a distance of about 20 ft. As they learn to execute it properly using either hand, gradually increase the distance.
2. One player can practice this pass alone by aiming at a spot on a wall.

Two-Hand Overhead Pass

The two-hand overhead pass is generally used for passing the ball over the head of a defensive player. Although coaches once considered this pass a cardinal sin, when used with caution it is an effective way to get the ball across a zone defense to an open player.

Performance Description

1. Hold the ball directly over the head in both hands, with the fingers spread, the thumbs behind the ball, and the wrists cocked (Figure 7.3).
2. Bring both arms forward, shift the weight toward the intended receiver, and snap the wrists.
3. On the release, the ball should roll off the two index fingers and the palms should turn to the outside.
4. Follow through with the fingers extended toward the receiver.

Common Errors

1. Holding the ball with the palms of the hands rather than the fingertips
2. Bringing the ball too far behind the head before beginning the forward movement
3. Not snapping the wrist enough on the longer passes

Figure 7.3
Two-hand (overhead) pass

Teaching Tips

1. Students should begin with short passes and gradually increase the distance.
2. Emphasize snapping the wrists to give more impetus to the ball.
3. This pass can be used in any of the previous pass drills.

Other Passes

Some advanced basketball players use several additional passes, including the lob, tip-out, behind-the-back, over-the-shoulder, and others. Although players may choose to work individually on executing these special passes, they are less likely to be used in game situations than are other passes. Most of the great players concentrate on executing the fundamental passes to perfection. We suggest teaching only those fundamental passes to larger groups.

ADVANCED DRIBBLING SKILLS

All players must be able to dribble at full speed with either hand if they are going to become serious participants in basketball. Those players who wish to improve their game and participate at even higher levels should learn additional dribbling maneuvers.

Change of Pace Dribble

To execute the change of pace dribble, a player need only change the speed at which he or she is moving while dribbling the ball. Because it makes the job of the defensive player more difficult, the change of pace is often used as an effective technique for advancing the ball into front court or moving toward the basket to create a scoring possibility.

Performance Description

1. With the right hand, dribble down the court at full speed.
2. At midcourt, suddenly stop moving forward, raise the trunk, slide the hand to the top of the ball, and come to an almost complete stop while maintaining the dribble.
3. While dribbling at a standstill or slowly advancing, suddenly push off with the right foot, accelerate, and continue dribbling with the right hand at full speed toward the basket.
4. Repeat the above procedure using the left-handed dribble.

Common Errors

1. Losing control of the ball when forward motion is stopped
2. Overrunning the dribble—running past the ball

Teaching Tips

1. Have students practice the change of pace dribble several times, moving the length of the floor.
2. A lay-up shot may be taken at the end of the dribble to combine the dribbling technique with a fundamental shot.

Crossover Dribble

When a player is closely guarded or overplayed to the dribbling side, the crossover dribble is a technique for changing direction quickly. When executing the crossover, keep the ball low to protect it from the defensive opponent.

Performance Description

1. While dribbling with the right hand, push the ball to the floor in front of the body so that the rebound will come to the left side (Figure 7.4a).
2. Simultaneously, step in front of the defensive player with the right foot (Figure 7.4b).
3. With the left hand, receive the ball on a short bounce as it rebounds from the floor and continue dribbling (Figure 7.4c).
4. Dribbling with the left hand, reverse the procedure.

Figure 7.4a

Figure 7.4b

Figure 7.4c

Figure 7.4
Crossover dribble

Common Errors

1.   Dribbling the ball too high
2.   Pushing the ball too far to the left, causing the ball to hit the foot

Teaching Tips

1.   When teaching the crossover, have the students begin at a walk and gradually increase their speed.
2.   Emphasize that the student requires a lot of practice before being able to use this movement to protect the ball from the opponent.

Drill

Crossover Dribble Drill

Place a chair in the area of the free throw line. Line the students up in single file at midcourt. Each student in turn dribbles to the chair, crossover dribbles to the left hand, drives to the basket, and shoots a left-handed lay-up. Students repeat the process using the opposite hand.

Reverse Dribble

Players use the reverse dribble to protect the ball and continue dribbling while reversing the direction of travel. The body of the dribbler is kept between the ball and the defensive opponent. The reverse dribble is usually performed when a defensive opponent is guarding the dribbler closely and is overplaying in the direction the dribbler is moving.

Performance Description

1.   While dribbling to the right, stop moving forward and place the weight on the left foot. Keep the knees bent and the body low (Figure 7.5).
2.   Swing the right foot backward, quickly turning the back to the defensive player.
3.   While turning, change the dribble to the left hand.
4.   Continue dribbling to the left, keeping the body between the ball and the defensive player.

Common Errors

1.   Straightening the body on the turn
2.   Switching the dribbling hand too late
3.   Palming the ball when changing dribbling hands

Teaching Tips

1.   Students should walk through the movements a few times before speeding up the procedure.
2.   Emphasize the importance of protecting the ball with the body.
3.   Have the students practice the dribble with each hand.

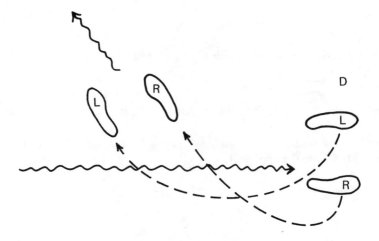

Figure 7.5
Footwork for reverse dribble

Drill

Reverse Dribble Drill

Using a square formed by the sideline, the baseline, the free throw line extended, and the free throw lane, have each student start in the corner of the floor and dribble around the inside perimeter of the square, using a reverse dribble at each corner. Students repeat drill several times using the right hand, then dribble in the opposite direction using the left hand.

ADVANCED SHOOTING SKILLS

While all players must learn to execute properly the lay-up shot, the jump shot, and the free throw, more advanced players should be able to demonstrate variations of the basic shots as well as some additional shots.

Inverted Lay-up Shot

The mechanics of the inverted lay-up are similar to those of regular lay-up shot. The inverted version is used when the offensive player has an opportunity to drive angularly to the basket but is prevented from placing the ball against the near side of the backboard. Instead, the driving player goes underneath the front edge of the rim and lays the ball against the board on the opposite side.

This shot can be used successfully when the defensive player, intent on preventing a lay-up on the strong side, overplays to the near side of the basket—allowing the shooter to attempt an inverted lay-up.

Performance Description

1. From a point along the left side of the free throw line extended and about midway between the sideline and the circle, dribble toward the basket with the left hand.
2. On entering the free throw lane, use the crossover dribble to switch the dribble to the right hand.
3. Go underneath the front edge of the rim, starting the leap from the left foot while passing under the rim.
4. On beginning the leap, turn the body toward the basket and shoot a right-handed lay-up.
5. Reverse the procedure for left-handed inverted lay-ups.

Common Errors

1. Starting the leap for the lay-up too soon
2. Starting the leap for the lay-up too late
3. Failure to turn the body toward the basket before releasing the shot

Teaching Tips

1. Review the mechanics of the lay-up.
2. Insist that the students turn the body toward the basket on the shot.
3. Since the body will be going away from the basket when the shot is released, be sure students understand the importance of beginning the leap under the basket.

Reverse Lay-up Shot

An offensive player using the reverse lay-up drives along the baseline, goes completely under the basket, and lays the ball back over the head onto the backboard. This shot is often used when the area under the basket is congested. Because the shooter is going away from the basket and away from the defensive opponent, this shot is more difficult to defend against than the regular lay-up.

Performance Description

1. Using the right hand, dribble along the baseline from left to right. Go underneath the basket.
2. While passing under the basket, begin to leap upward from the left foot. Control the ball with both hands.
3. With both hands, bring the ball upward, directly in front of the body. Stretch upward.
4. Release the ball with a twist of the right hand, turning it so that it spins clockwise. Place the ball against the backboard about midway between the edge of the board and the edge of the rim, and about 12 in. above the level of the basket. The spin, or English, will cause the ball to reverse into the basket.
5. Reverse the above procedure to shoot a left-handed reverse lay-up.

Common Errors

1. Starting the leap too soon and hitting the underside of the rim with the ball
2. Failure to put a spin on the ball as it is released
3. Failure to place the ball high enough on the backboard

Teaching Tips

1. Before practicing this shot, students should simply stand under the basket and work on spinning the ball up against the backboard.
2. Start the students at about half speed and allow them to increase their speed gradually as they improve.

Hook Shot

The hook shot is probably the most difficult shot to defend against and, for most players, the most difficult shot to master. All advanced players should learn to use the hook shot, particularly the taller players who are often near the basket. It can be a valuable offensive weapon.

Performance Description

1. With the back to the basket, the feet parallel, and the body balanced, hold the ball in both hands at waist level.
2. For a right-hand shot, hold the right hand under the ball, step on the left foot, and extend the right arm fully away from the body.
3. While stepping onto the left foot, look over the left shoulder and turn the body sideways to the basket. Focus the eyes on the point of aim.
4. Bring the right hand upward in a swinging motion toward the basket.
5. Release the ball at its apex. As the ball rolls off the index finger, snap the wrist for the follow-through.
6. Complete the turn until facing the basket, and land in a balanced position on both feet, ready to rebound.

Common Errors

1. Failure to maintain body balance throughout the shot
2. Failure to look toward the basket before releasing the ball
3. Allowing the ball to rest on the palm during the shot rather than on the fingertips
4. Slinging the ball rather than shooting it—releasing the ball too soon

Teaching Tips

1. Be sure that students begin learning this shot close to the basket and move away only after mastering the short shots.
2. Maximum range for this shot is 12-15 ft from the basket. Do not allow students to make a hook shot from a greater distance.

TWO- AND THREE-PLAYER OFFENSIVE PATTERNS

There are a number of two- and three-player patterns that enable one player to elude the defensive opponent and secure a good shot at the basket. The most common of the two-player patterns are the front door cut, the back door cut, the give and go, and the pick and roll. The two most common three-player patterns are the double split and the pick away from the ball.

Front Door Cut (Figure 7.6)

Performance Description

1. O_2 fakes opponent D out of position, then cuts in front of opponent (on ball side) and breaks toward the basket.
2. O_1 passes the ball to O_2 when open.

Back Door Cut (Figure 7.7)

Performance Description

1. When the defensive opponent is overplaying to the side toward the ball, O_2 fakes in the direction of the ball, then cuts behind opponent toward the basket.
2. O_1 passes the ball to O_2 when open.

Give and Go (Split Cut)

Performance Description

1. O_1 passes the ball to O_2 and breaks past the defensive opponent toward the basket. This can be a front door cut, a back door cut, or a split cut, as shown in Figure 7.8.
2. O_2 returns the ball to O_1 as O_1 becomes open.

Pick and Roll (Figure 7.9)

Performance Description

1. O_1 passes the ball to O_2 and sets a pick at the side of D, O_2's defensive opponent.
2. Once the pick is set, O_2 dribbles past O_1 close enough to run the defensive opponent into the pick set by O_1.

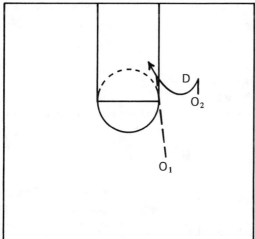

Figure 7.6
Front door cut

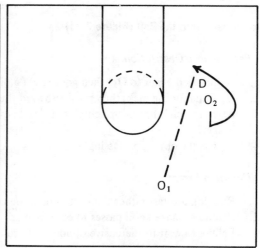

Figure 7.7
Back door cut

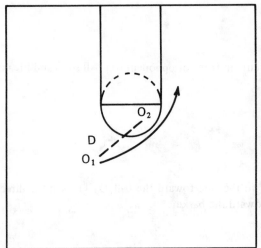

Figure 7.8
Give and go (split cut)

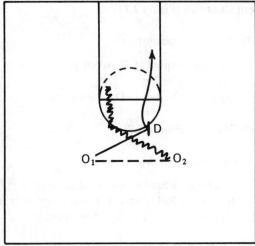

Figure 7.9
Pick and roll

3. O_2's defensive opponent makes contact with O_2; O_1 does a rear pivot, opening to the ball, and rolls toward the basket.
4. O_2 either takes the ball to the basket or passes to O_1, depending on the movement of the defense.

Double Split (Figure 7.10)

Performance Description

1. O_1 passes the ball to O_3 and cuts toward the basket, passing in front of O_3.
2. O_2 cuts for the basket, passing behind O_1 and in front of O_3.
3. O_3 has the option of passing the ball to O_1 or O_2, driving for the basket, or turning and shooting the ball.

Pick Away From the Ball (Figure 7.11)

Performance Description

1. O_3 passes the ball to O_2, then goes to set a pick for O_1.
2. O_1 waits for the pick, then breaks toward the basket.
3.   After the pick has been completed, O_3 does a rear pivot, opening toward O_1, and rolls to the basket.
4. O_2 has the option of passing to O_1 or O_3.

Common Errors

1.   Running too fast rather than running in the correct pattern
2.   Failure to make good passes to open player
3.   Failure to wait for defensive opponent to run into the pick

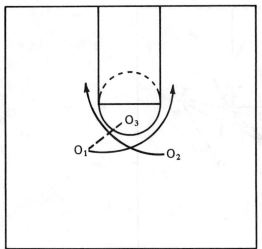

Figure 7.10
Double split

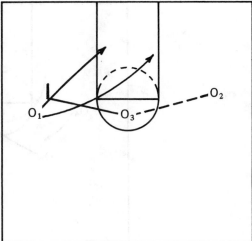

Figure 7.11
Pick away from the ball

Teaching Tips

1. Emphasize the need for good passes.
2. Point out the importance of running good patterns before going full speed.
3. Demonstrate the need to set good picks.

TEAM OFFENSE

The two basic types of offense are those used against the player-to-player defense and those used against the zone defenses. Always teach player-to-player offense first, and be sure students have mastered it before starting on zone offense.

The most important consideration in developing a team offense is to keep it simple. Remember that there are no secrets in basketball: the team that is best drilled in fundamentals and that makes the fewest mistakes usually wins.

A good offense is one that allows all five players an opportunity to score or handle the ball each time the offense is run. This provides an incentive for each player to put forth the best effort. If an offensive pattern gives a player no opportunity to handle the ball or score, that player will ease up.

Although offensive patterns are numerous, we will describe only one simple pattern for each type of offense.

Player-to-Player Offense (Figure 7.12)

Player-to-player offense was the bread and butter of the powerhouse teams of coach Adolph Rupp at the University of Kentucky. This offense is ideal in that it involves all players, provides several

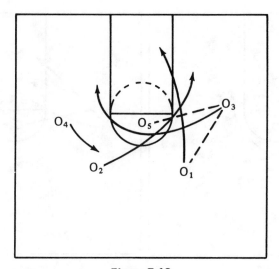

Figure 7.12
Player-to-player offensive pattern

options depending on the defensive action, and can be started from either side of the floor. If properly executed, this offensive pattern will result in scoring opportunities in which the likelihood of a goal is high.

Performance Description

1. Player O_1 passes the ball to O_3 and breaks directly toward the basket. If O_1 is open, O_3 may return the ball to O_1.
2. If O_1 is not open, O_1 will continue under the basket and go back out to the midcourt area for defense, in case the opponent gains possession of the ball.
3. If O_3 does not give the ball back to O_1, then the ball is passed to O_5. O_3 follows the ball across the floor, goes past O_5, and breaks toward the basket.
4. Player O_2 breaks toward the basket on the same side as O_1, then immediately moves directly behind O_3 near the position of O_5. This allows O_2 to get free of defensive opponent.
5. Player O_4 follows route of O_2, also passing close to O_3 to lose the defensive opponent.
6. Player O_5 has several options: (a) pass to O_2, (b) pass to O_3, (c) pass to O_4, (d) turn and shoot, (e) drive to the basket, or (f) pass out to O_1 and set up the offensive pattern again.

Common Errors

1. Failure to coordinate movements with teammates properly
2. Predetermining which player will get the ball
3. Failure to pass closely enough to teammates to pick off the defensive opponent.
4. Failure to continue running pattern until complete, thereby clogging up the middle

Teaching Tips

1. Set a team on the court and have students walk through the pattern at least once for each option available. No defense should be used.
2. Students should run through the offensive pattern at full speed at least six times from each side of the floor. Still use no defense.
3. Run the offensive pattern against a no-hands defense. Require the defense to keep their hands behind their backs while attempting to stay with their opponents.
4. Run the offensive pattern against a full defense.

Zone Offense

When setting up a zone offense, the instructor should examine the alignment of each type of zone defense and determine the weakness of that particular defense. The four basic techniques of attacking zone defenses are the overload, the screen, the cut, and the rotation. Whatever the technique, the primary requirements for beating any zone defense are patience and quick movement of the ball.

The most commonly used zone defenses are the 2-3 zone, the 3-2 zone, and the 1-3-1 zone. The 2-1-2 zone, also often used, is an adaptation of the 2-3 and the 3-2 zones. To attack the zones, two basic offensive alignments, the 1-3-1 offensive set and the overload set (Figure 7.13), are recommended. From either of these offensive formations, a team may use any of the four basic techniques of attack.

We will describe here only one example of each offensive technique. These examples show the 1-3-1 offensive set against a 2-3 zone defense, perhaps the most frequently used zone defense.

Overload Offense (Figure 7.14)

The overload offense places offensive players in and around the zone in such a way that the offensive players outnumber the defensive players in a certain area of the court. Continual rapid movement of the ball into that area eventually results in a good shot at the basket.

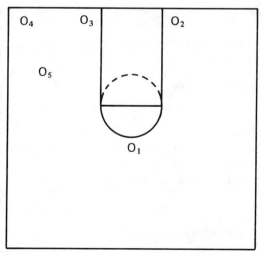

Figure 7.13
Overload set

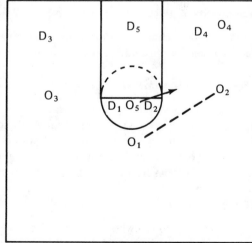

Figure 7.14
Overload offense

Performance Description

1. Player O_1 passes the ball to O_2.
2. Player O_2 may pass to either O_4 or O_5.
3. Players O_2, O_4, and O_5 outnumber D_4 and D_5. The open player takes the shot.

Screen Offense (Figure 7.15)

Any zone defense can be screened successfully. Defensive players have an assigned area to cover. By moving an offensive player or players into a position that prevents the defensive player from getting to an assigned area quickly, the offense can secure some good shots at the basket.

Performance Description

1. Player O_1 passes the ball to O_5.
2. Player O_2 sets a screen on D_2.
3. Player O_1 breaks behind D_2.
4. Player O_5 passes to O_1 for the shot.

Cut Offense (Figure 7.16)

Players using the cut offense cut into the open areas vacated by defensive players as they shift with the ball. To employ this effective method of attack, observe the defense to find the open area, quickly move an offensive player into that area, then get the ball to that player.

Performance Description

1. Player O_1 passes to O_2.
2. Player O_1 cuts into the area vacated by D_2.
3. Player O_2 passes to O_1 for the shot.

Rotation Offense (Figure 7.17)

The rotation technique is essentially a combination of the overload and the cut. It is particularly effective when the three middle players are used in a 1-3-1 set.

Performance Description

1. Player O_1 passes to O_2.
2. Player O_2 passes to O_4 and breaks toward the basket.
3. Player O_5 moves into the spot previously occupied by O_2, while O_3 moves into the spot previously occupied by O_5. Player O_2 goes to the spot vacated by O_3.
4. Player O_4 looks for the open player and immediately gets the ball to that player.

Common Errors

1. Passes made too slowly, allowing the defense to shift into proper position
2. Impatience on the part of the offense
3. Failure to move into the open areas
4. Failure to take the good shot when available

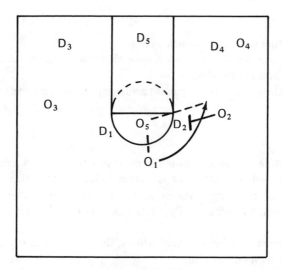

Figure 7.15
Screen offense

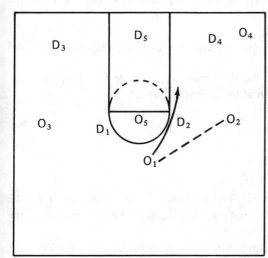

Figure 7.16
Cut offense

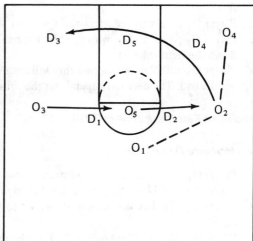

Figure 7.17
Rotation offense

Teaching Tips

1. Insist that the students make good, quick passes.
2. As the ball moves and the defense shifts, have all students freeze on a predetermined signal. Point out the weak areas of the defense.
3. Insist that the offensive players be patient and continue to pass the ball until a good shot is available.

Fast Break Offense

The fast break is an offensive tactic designed to maneuver the ball into scoring position so quickly that the defense either is not in position or is outnumbered by the offensive players. Teams that employ the fast break may find opportunities to do so after a missed shot by the opponent, on a steal or an intercepted pass, and occasionally, after a successful field goal or free throw by the opponent.

Although there are several fast break combinations, the most frequently executed are the three-on-two pattern and the two-on-one pattern.

Three-on-Two Fast Break (Figure 7.18)

Performance Description

1. Player O_1 rebounds the ball and passes it out to O_2. Player O_4 starts down the left side of the floor.
2. Player O_3 breaks to the middle of the court.
3. Player O_2 passes to O_3, who dribbles the ball down the center of the floor. Player O_2 continues down the right sideline.
4. Player O_3 dribbles to the free throw line and has the option of passing to O_1 or O_4, or shooting the ball. The decision depends on the action of the defensive players.

Two-on-One Fast Break (Figure 7.19)

Performance Description

1. Player O_1 rebounds the ball and passes it out to O_2.
2. Player O_2 dribbles the ball down the right sideline while O_3 breaks down the left side. Player O_2 also has the option of passing to O_3 and allowing O_3 to dribble the ball down the court.
3. When the player dribbling the ball is about even with the free throw line, he or she has the option of passing to a teammate, driving to the basket for a lay-up, or making a short jump shot. The player's choice depends on the action that the defensive player takes.

Common Errors

1. Failure of the rebounder to get the outlet pass quickly to the side
2. Failure of the ball handler to make the defense commit itself
3. Failure to use the proper option

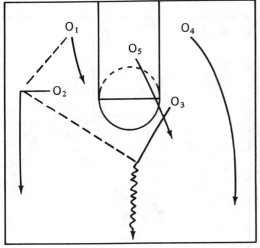

Figure 7.18
Three-on-two fast break

Figure 7.19
Two-on-one fast break

Teaching Tips

1. Be sure the students understand that the fast break cannot be forced. If no opportunity occurs for the fast break, hold up, and set up the regular offense.
2. The key to a successful fast break is the speed with which the outlet pass is made after the rebound.
3. Emphasize the importance of good passes. Fast-breaking teams must be able to handle the ball well.

Out-of-Bounds Situations

Out-of-bounds plays are special plays designed to get the ball into the court within 5 sec. Because of the lapse in action, however, these situations often present an opportunity to score quickly and easily.

Most teams have an out-of-bounds play for the front court baseline and one for the front court sideline. These plays usually have two or more options. Figure 7.20 shows a commonly used baseline play and Figure 7.21 a commonly used sideline play.

Baseline Play

Performance Description

1. Player O_2 sets a pick for O_3, who then breaks toward the ball. Player O_2 then executes a rear pivot and breaks toward the basket.
2. Player O_4 sets a pick for O_5, who then breaks to the position formerly occupied by O_4.

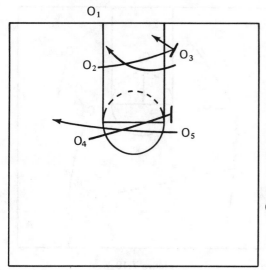

Figure 7.20
Baseline out-of-bounds play

Figure 7.21
Sideline out-of-bounds play

3.   Player O_1 has the option of passing the ball in bounds to O_2 or O_3 in scoring position. If the closer players are well guarded, player O_1 may avoid possible interception by passing to O_5.

Sideline Play

Performance Description

1.   Player O_5 sets a pick for O_4, who then breaks toward the basket for a lob pass.
2.   Player O_2 sets a pick for O_3, who immediately breaks toward the ball. Player O_2 then executes a rear pivot, opening up to the ball.
3.   Player O_1 may pass to O_4 for a shot, or to O_2 or O_3 to get the ball in bounds.

Common Errors

1.   Improperly set picks
2.   Failure of the player for whom the pick is set to maneuver opponent into the pick
3.   Failure of the player making the throw-in to let the play develop

Teaching Tips

1.   Be sure each student understands all of the options.
2.   Emphasize that the primary purpose of the play is to get the ball safely in bounds.
3.   Review with the students the proper procedure for setting picks.

TEAM DEFENSE

The importance of teaching sound team defense cannot be overemphasized. The ability and willingness to play defense is often the difference between a good team and a mediocre team. To sell the concept of good defense to the players, the instructor must convince them that the defensive star is just as valuable as the offensive star.

Defense must be taught as a team concept. If one player fails to play sound defense, the entire team suffers. When all five players apply sound techniques of individual defense, their coordinated efforts result in sound team defense.

The two basic types of defense are the player-to-player defense and the zone defense. In player-to-player defense, each player guards a specific opponent, regardless of where that opponent may go. In zone defense, each defensive player guards against the ball in a specific area of the court.

Player-to-Player Defense

Player-to-player defense is the mainstay of most winning teams. Any team that cannot play a sound player-to-player defense eventually meets defeat. Regardless of how well a team plays zone defense, a time comes late in a game when the defense must come out and pressure the ball to attempt to gain possession.

Player-to-player defense allows the defensive team to make assignments in accordance with the opponents' height, position, speed, and shooting ability.

Most teams use several basic principles of player-to-player defense. These include:

1. Maintain a position between the assigned opponent and the basket, except when guarding a pivot player in a low post position near the basket. In that area, front the opponent or stay between the opponent and the ball.
2. Always "point" or pressure the ball. A defensive player must guard the opponent with the ball closely, particularly when within shooting distance.
3. Prevent the high-percentage shot. Good defensive teams seldom give up a lay-up shot or a short jump shot within 10 ft of the basket. When an offensive player eludes the defensive opponent, all defensive players are responsible to help out.
4. Prevent the second shot. An old axiom is that the team that controls the backboards wins the game. Every defensive player must block out an opponent from the backboard to reduce the possibility of offensive rebounds and second shots.
5. Protect the baseline. Do not allow the opponent to drive along the baseline to the basket.
6. Keep the ball out of the pivot area, where defending against a good player with the ball is extremely difficult.
7. Handle the screens. If switching is to be used, these techniques must be practiced. Switching involves the exchange of defensive assignments while play continues; it is a way of combating picks that the opponent sets. Some teachers instruct their students to switch automatically each time two offensive players exchange positions on the floor; others prefer their players to switch only when one of the defensive players may be screened or otherwise hindered from maintaining the normal defensive position. Switches are called by the defensive players involved in them. If switching is not to be used, practice sliding through or going over the top of the screen.
8. Talk on defense. Talking between teammates on defense is imperative. Players must be warned of screens and picks and advised of the action to be taken.

When sound individual techniques are combined with these principles, the result should be a solid team defense.

Zone Defense

Zone defense differs from player-to-player defense in that it is focused on the players rather than on the ball. The strong points for zone defenses are: (1) they allow the defensive team strong rebounding positions, (2) players are positioned to employ the fast break after gaining a rebound, and (3) they are effective against poor outside shooting teams. The weaknesses of zone defenses are: (1) they are susceptible to good outside shooting teams, (2) they are generally weaker against a good fast-breaking team, and (3) when behind in scoring, defensive players must come farther out on the court to force the team in control of the ball to make a play.

The basic zone defenses are the 2-3 zone (Figure 7.22), the 3-2 zone (Figure 7.23), and the 1-3-1 zone (Figure 7.24). These basic zones have several adaptations, including the 1-2-2 zone and the 2-1-2 zone.

As in player-to-player defense, most teachers employ certain principles. The principles of zone defense are:

1. Get into position quickly. Immediately on transition from offense to defense, each defensive player must go to an assigned position as quickly as possible to prevent a fast break.
2. Maintain a good fundamental defensive stance. The defense must shift rapidly as the opponent passes the ball around. A correct stance enables the defensive player to move quickly.
3. Keep the hands up. Holding the hands high in the air helps obstruct the vision of the offensive players and often enables the defensive player to deflect passes.
4. Talk with teammates. Teammates must be informed of movement behind them and warned of picks or screens being set.
5. Never turn away from the ball. The attention of the defensive players should be on the ball, as they must shift with each movement of the ball.
6. Prevent the second shot. Each defender must screen off the nearest opponent from the backboard to prevent an offensive rebound or second shot.

For a team to develop a good zone defense, each player must have good fundamental individual defensive techniques. The players also must have a good knowledge of the game of basketball; the ability to anticipate the offensive action enhances the effectiveness of the zone defense.

PROJECTS FOR PROSPECTIVE TEACHERS

1. Design and explain at least one drill for each of the following skills: inverted lay-up, reverse lay-up, one-hand pass, hook pass, crossover dribble, and reverse dribble.
2. Develop a 40-min lesson plan on offensive techniques, including time for taking roll, warm-up exercises, demonstrations, and evaluation.

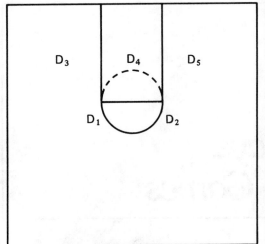

Figure 7.22
2-3 Zone

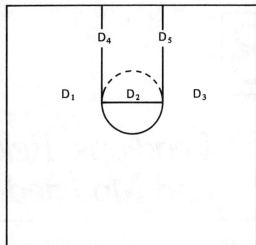

Figure 7.23
3-2 Zone

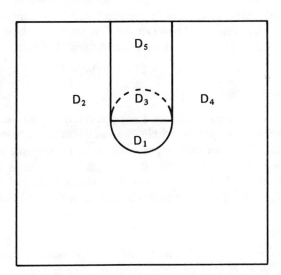

Figure 7.24
1-3-1 Zone

8

Lead-ups, Relays, and Modified Games

LEAD-UP GAMES

Lead-up games are a good way to teach basic skills to beginning level players; they afford opportunities for the development of specific skills without the complexity of the official game of basketball. By combining elements of fun and competition with the application of skills, lead-ups make repetitive skill practice interesting for the participants. Because the games vary in scope (using one skill or multiple skills), difficulty, equipment requirements, and the number of players accommodated, an instructor must select those that best suit the situation and skills of the participants. In the following games, young players or players who are afraid to catch a hard ball may use playground balls or volleyballs.

Count Passes

A lead-up game such as count passes helps to develop accurate passing and defensive skills. Divide the class into two teams. Scatter all players within one half of the court. Start the game with a jump ball in the restraining circle. The team gaining possession must try to make as many varied and consecutive passes as possible. The opponents use player-to-player defense to attempt to intercept a pass and gain possession of the ball. Official rules determining fouls and ball-handling violations apply. The official counts accurate passes out loud; the team with the most consecutive passes wins.

Volleyball-Basketball-Softball

Students can use the game of volleyball-basketball-softball to work on shooting and passing skills, as well as teamwork. Arrange bases on a basketball court in a diamond formation. Allow a distance of 30 ft between bases; place home plate directly under one basket. Divide the class into two teams with one team at bat and the other in the field. Use a rubber playground ball or volleyball. Each batter attempts to: (1) bat the ball with the hand into the playing field, which is determined by extensions of the first and third baselines, and (2) score a run by consecutively touching all four bases before the fielding team makes three consecutive successful passes and scores a goal at the opposite end basket. Softball rules, including three outs, foul balls, and missing bases, apply. The team with the most runs at the end of seven innings wins.

In one variation, a basketball is substituted for the volleyball and thrown overhand into the playing area. If a kickball is used instead, it is kicked instead of batted into the field.

Flag Dribble

Flag dribble helps to develop controlled dribbling ability. Players are scattered within one half of the court and equipped with a flag (tucked in the back of the belt or waistband) and a ball. While dribbling in bounds, each player tries to pull the flag or knock the ball from another player. A player is eliminated who has the flag pulled, loses control of the dribble, or touches out-of-bounds. The sole remaining player is declared the winner.

Dribble Tag

Dribble tag helps students to work on dribbling ability. While dribbling a ball and moving within a confined area, each player attempts to tag another player. Tagged players are disqualified. The one remaining player wins.

Five Passes

The game of five passes develops passing and cutting skills. Two teams of five players each compete in a half-court area. Each team tries to complete five consecutive passes to score 1 point. The game begins with a jump ball between opponents in the restraining circle. A player may not pass back to the person from whom he or she received the ball. Regulation rules determine ball-handling violations and fouls. No dribbling is allowed. If a fumble occurs, a new count begins. After a point is scored, the other team takes the ball out-of-bounds at the center line.

Six-Zone Basketball

Six-zone basketball allows students to practice passing, catching, shooting, and guarding skills. Divide the court into six zones, with division lines extending across the court (Figure 8.1). Lines designating end zones are 8 ft from a spot directly under each basket. Other zones are about 18 ft long.

Two or three players from one team are placed in every other zone so that team A's guards are at one end, team B's forwards are in the next zone, team A's centers are in the adjacent third zone (near center court), and so forth.

The game starts with a center jump ball. Each team then tries to pass the ball from its centers to its forwards, who attempt to score field goals worth 2 points from within their zone. After a score, the opposing guards put the ball in play from out-of-bounds behind the end line. Violations include not passing the ball to each zone when advancing the ball, traveling, holding the ball more than 5 sec, and stepping on or over any division lines or court boundaries. For any violation, the closest member of the opposing team is awarded the ball out-of-bounds at the sideline nearest the spot of the violation. Players rotate positions at the end of each playing period—guards change to forwards, forwards to centers, and centers to guards.

Partner Shooting

Partner shooting helps students to learn to shoot quickly from different areas of the court. Use four to six baskets around the court, with a team of two or three players at each basket. The object of the game is to score as many points as possible in 2 min.

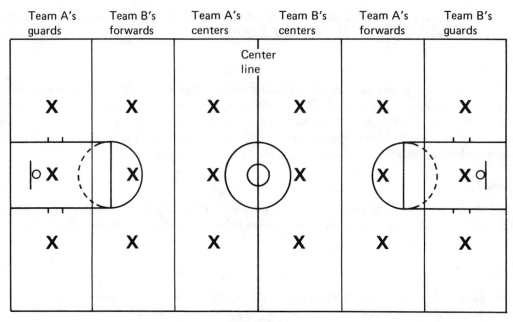

Figure 8.1
Six-zone basketball

The first player from each group takes a shot from a designated spot on the court. The shooter follows the shot to the basket and makes any necessary follow-ups until successful. The ball is quickly passed back to the next player, who also attempts a shot from the designated spot, and so on. A successful first shot scores 3 points, a first attempt tip-in 3 points, a second attempt tip-in 2 points, and a follow-up shot 1 point. After a 2-min contest, each team rotates clockwise to a different basket from which shots must be taken from a different angle on the court. Each team's score is the combined total of points made at all baskets.

Horse

The lead-up game horse gives students an opportunity to develop varied shooting ability. Each group is assigned to a basket, and the players establish a shooting order. The first player shoots from any position on the court. If the shot is successful, the next player must attempt the same shot. If the second player fails to make the shot, he or she receives an H. If the shot is made, the next player must also attempt this shot. If unsuccessful, the third player receives an H. Players receive a letter each time a repeated goal attempt is missed. After a goal is missed, the next player in line may execute any shot from any position on the court, with no penalty for a missed shot. After all the others are disqualified for spelling "horse," the winner is the only remaining player.

Basket Team Ball

Students can practice making quick shots by playing basket team ball. Players are divided into as many teams as available baskets. Each team forms a single line behind the free throw line. On a signal, the first player in line shoots for a basket. The second player recovers the ball and attempts a shot from the spot of recovery. The remaining players follow this pattern. After making an attempt, each shooter moves to the end of the line, no matter whether the shot was successful. Goals count 1 point. Players continue until a team has scored 20 points.

Team Twenty-one

The game of team twenty-one helps students to work on free throw and lay-up shooting skills and to practice taking rebounds. Groups of three to five players are stationed at each basket, with one player at the free throw line and the others in the free throw lane spaces. The player at the free throw line shoots until he or she misses a shot. Other players vie for the rebound. The player who recovers the rebound attempts a follow-up shot, while surrounding players try to block the ball. A player who scores a goal from the rebound becomes the next free throw shooter. Other players rotate one lane position clockwise. If the field goal attempt is unsuccessful, the free throw shooter remains at the free throw line. Free throws count 1 point and field goals 2 points; the winner is the first player to score 21 points.

Five-Three-One

Students can improve their free throw, short-range, and lay-up shooting ability by playing five-three-one. Players line up behind the free throw line. The first player attempts a free throw worth 5 points, takes a second shot from wherever the ball is recovered worth 3 points, and takes a third shot—a lay-up—worth 1 point. A player is allowed three shots per turn, whatever the success or failure of the shots. The first player to score 50 points wins. Teams can compete with each other if each team is assigned a different basket.

Around the World

Playing around the world allows students to practice shooting skills. Eight shooting spots are designated around the key area shown in the diagram (Figure 8.2). Players line up at position 1. The first player makes a shot, and if successful, moves to position 2 for the next attempt. As long as no shot is missed, the player continues to rotate around the key. A player who has missed a shot has two options—stay at that position and wait for the next turn after other players have shot, or chance taking another shot from that position. If the chance is successful, the player continues around the world. If the chance is unsuccessful, the player must start back at position 1 on the next turn.

Pinball

By playing pinball, students can work on passing skills, ball handling, and teamwork as well as their knowledge of basketball rules. Draw a circle 6 ft in diameter at both ends of the playing court and place an Indian club in each circle. The object of the game is to knock down the opponent's Indian club. While standing in the designated circle, one goalie from each team guards that team's pin. Other players scatter around the court. If any player other than a goalie steps inside the circle, or if any player fouls an opponent, the opponent is given a free chance to knock down the pin from the free throw line. During a free throw the goalie must be out of the circle; all other players line up on the free throw lane line until the attempt is completed. The ball is moved down the floor according to regular basketball rules. The team that scores the most pin knockdowns is the winner.

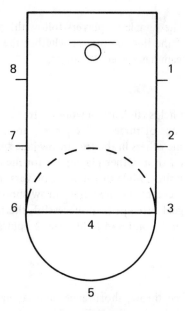

Figure 8.2
Around the world

Golf Basketball

Golf basketball is a way to practice shooting from various parts of the court (Figure 8.3). Draw nine circles, each with a 4-ft radius, in an arc around the basket from the left to the right corner of the floor. Each player attempts a set shot from the first circle, or tee. A player who scores on the first attempt in a circle is awarded a hole-in-one and has 1 point deducted from his or her score. If the shot is missed, the player is allowed a second attempt. If the player scores on the second try, he or she is assessed 2 strokes. If the player misses both shots, the penalty is the addition of 2 more points to the score, making the score for that hole a 4.

After each player has attempted shots from the first tee, all the players move to the second circle and attempt to make a basket from this position. Players continue until they have played all nine holes. The player with the lowest score wins.

Twenty-one

The game of twenty-one helps to develop shooting skills. Three to eight players line up in single file behind the free throw line. Each player shoots a long shot from the line, followed by a short shot from within two steps of wherever the ball is recovered. The player may continue to shoot the long and short shot sequence until a shot is missed: the player then loses the right to continue shooting and the next player takes a turn.

Successful long shots score 2 points and short shots 1. The first player to score 21 points wins. In a variation of the game, teams compete against each other and each player contributes to the group score.

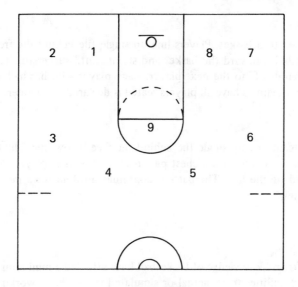

Figure 8.3
Golf basketball

Call That Number

Students can use call that number to work on dribbling, lay-up, or close-range shooting ability. Divide the class into two teams and assign each team to a sideline. Place two basketballs in the center circle in deck tennis rings (to prevent rolling). Each team numbers off so that each player has an assigned number. If one team has an extra player, one player on the opposing team can respond to two numbers. As the instructor calls out a number, the two opponents rush to the center circle, grab a ball, dribble to opposite baskets, and shoot until successful. After making a shot, each player quickly dribbles back to the center circle and returns the ball to the ring. The team of the first player to return the ball to the circle is awarded 1 point. The instructor then calls another number. To insure each player an opportunity, a record should be kept of numbers called.

In one variation of call that number, several balls are placed in the center circle. The instructor calls out two or three numbers at a time. The first team to return all the balls to the circle is awarded 1 point. In another variation, chairs are placed in single file from the center circle to each basket. After taking the ball from the center circle, each player weaves around the chairs to the basket and back.

RELAYS

Most drills can be converted into relays suitable for students of various skill levels. Like lead-up games, relays motivate students by incorporating an element of competition into the practice skills. We have included two sample relays suitable for elementary school children.

Lay-up Relay

Each team is assigned to a basket. Players line up single file behind the free throw line. On a signal, the first player dribbles toward the basket and shoots until successful. The player then dribbles back to the line and hands off to the next player. Each player who has had a turn sits down at the end of the line. The first team to have all players seated is declared the winner.

Dribble Relay

Players from each team line up single file behind the free throw line. The first player in each line dribbles to the end line and executes a chest pass back to the next player. After the pass, the first player runs to the end of the line. The pattern continues until all team members have returned to their lines.

MODIFIED GAMES

Once students' skills and knowledge of basketball have attained a minimum level, they are anxious to apply their acquired abilities to an actual or simulated game. When working with large groups or limited facilities, the instructor may modify the official game to maximize participation and enjoyment.

Scramble Basketball

Two teams, A and B, line up on opposite sidelines on one half of the court. Players on each team count off; three or fewer teammates take each number. The instructor calls out one of the numbers and tosses the ball against the backboard. Team members whose number is called rush toward the ball. The team that takes the rebound becomes the offensive team, and the opponents immediately assume defensive positions. The object of the game is to gain possession of the ball and score. Once a team has possession, regular half-court basketball rules apply. Free throws are awarded for all fouls. A 2-min time limit is set for each numbered group. Baskets count 2 points and free throws 1 point.

Line Basketball

Line basketball is designed to provide one-on-one offensive and defensive practice. One shooter and one defender take their positions at the top of the key. Other players line up along the end line and may receive passes from the shooter. The offensive player maneuvers, passing to the end line players at will and attempting to score. If a shot is missed, the player gaining the rebound dribbles the ball back to the top of the key and becomes the offensive player. The game continues until a basket is made. A player who has scored remains on the court as the defender; the player scored against moves to the end of the players along the end line, and the first player in line closest to the left sideline moves onto the court as the offensive player.

Half-Court Basketball

Half-court basketball uses only one basket and is played on half of the regulation basketball court. Each team is made up of five players, and with a few exceptions, official rules apply. The exceptions are:

1. The game is started with a jump ball in the restraining circle. Jumpers face opposing sidelines. The team gaining possession of the ball assumes offensive status, and the opponents assume defensive positions.
2. When a team intercepts the ball, offensive and defensive roles are immediately changed; the intercepting team must take the ball back to midcourt.
3. When the defensive team gains possession of the ball immediately after the opponents miss a field goal or free throw attempt, it must move the ball back to midcourt before attempting to shoot for a goal. A team taking an offensive rebound may shoot immediately without moving the ball to midcourt.
4. After a goal is made, the opponents of the shooting team put the ball in play from midcourt.
5. For out-of-bounds and ball-handling violations, the ball is awarded to the opponents out-of-bounds at the spot closest to where the violation occurred. The offended team may progress from that point without taking the ball back to midcourt.

Sideline Basketball

Three to five players from two teams are on the court. Each team is assigned a basket. Teammates stand on the sidelines, where they participate by catching and passing balls back to the on-court players and attempting to keep the ball in bounds.

To start the game and after each score, on-court players from each team line up on one end line. The instructor passes the ball to one of the players (generally an opponent of the scoring team) and the teams play regular basketball until a score is made or time expires (2–3 min per group is recommended), at which point new players replace those on the court.

Three-on-Three Basketball

Following regular basketball rules, two teams of three players each compete on one half of the court. The game begins with a jump ball in the restraining circle; opponents face opposite sidelines. When a score is made or the ball is recovered by the team on defense, the defensive team moves to center court and becomes the offensive team.

In a variation of three-on-three, a third team may be stationed out-of-bounds at the end line and take the floor: (1) after a predetermined number of points have been scored by one team or (2) after the defensive team recovers the ball and the offensive team rotates off the floor. In the second case, the third team rotates in as defenders, and the defensive team shifts to offense.

Four-on-Four Basketball

Four offensive players from one team and four defensive players from the other team take positions on half the court. Defensive players may play a box zone or player-to-player. Teammates of both teams are evenly distributed along opposite sidelines, as well as along the center line and end line. To begin the game, a starting offensive player at the center court line makes an unguarded pass to a teammate. On-court players must pass to sidelined teammates, who may not shoot or guard but who must pass back to teammates in bounds. When a basket is made (field goal or free throw), the starting players of both teams move out-of-bounds to the far end of their respective sidelines. The four players from each team who are closest to the center of the center line become the new players. The team that did not score is given the ball at the center line for a free throw-in.

If the defensive team gains possession of the ball, the players must pass or dribble the ball back to the center line for the free throw-in, and thus become the offensive team. Regulation rules govern fouls, violations, and jump balls.

Several additional rules insure the involvement of the sidelined players. On a missed free throw, the ball must be passed to a sidelined player before it can be passed back to a teammate at the center line to continue play. After a jump ball, the ball must be passed to a sidelined player who passes it out to a teammate at the center line. Out-of-bounds players make all end line and sideline throw-ins.

Winners Stay

Divide class into four or six teams of three to five players, depending on the number of baskets available. Station two teams at each basket. Half-court basketball rules apply with a time limit of 5 min. Winning teams stay at the basket, and losing teams rotate clockwise to the next basket and game.

If only two baskets are available, three teams may be stationed at a basket. Two teams play and the losing team rotates out, allowing the third team to rotate in for the next game.

PROJECTS FOR PROSPECTIVE TEACHERS

1. Design a basketball lead-up game appropriate for sixth-grade students and teach it to an upper elementary physical education class or a group of prospective elementary school teachers.
2. Design a class tournament for six teams using three baskets and modified game rules.

9

Evaluation

As mentioned in Chapter 2, the first step in planning a basketball unit is determining suitable psychomotor, cognitive, and affective objectives for the student to achieve. Periodically and at the end of each unit, the teacher should measure student performance according to the attainment of these objectives. Students may also want to assess their own achievement and improvement during the course of the unit.

Valid evaluative methods that discriminate among various levels of competence are vital for student assessment. To measure development in the three learning domains, instructors need performance tests, observation charts, statistics, written or verbal evaluations, and attitude scales.

Coaches often face the task of selecting the best prospective team members from a large number of hopefuls. During the season, continuous evaluation of individual and team performance is an integral part of the coaching process. Coaches and instructors who wish to identify better players and diagnose faulty performance can do so more objectively by administering various performance tests and recording and analyzing scrimmage or game statistics.

PSYCHOMOTOR ASSESSMENT

Performance Tests

Several batteries of performance tests, including from three to nine items, have been widely accepted as objective indicators of ability. When administered at the beginning of a basketball unit, these tests determine the initial level of skill of an individual or a group. This information can be used to classify students (ability grouping), establish expectations, plan lessons (according to instructional needs), and chart improvement (through comparisons with later scores). In athletics, performance test results coupled with analyses of scrimmage statistics can be instrumental in team selection by enabling the coach to reduce the number of candidates and evaluate the remaining players subjectively.

Two forms of organization that make the best use of facilities and expedite the administration of tests are: (1) rotating each group through a circuit in which student leaders administer a different test at each station and (2) having all groups perform the same test simultaneously while the instructor administers the test from a central location.

AAHPERD Skills Tests

The AAHPERD Skills Tests[1] is one battery of tests we recommend. The nine tests are designed to measure performance in the fundamental skills of basketball. The tests act as an incentive for the improvement of skills. To enable instructors to compare their students' scores, the tests are accompanied by national norms for boys and girls. Norms for each test are provided in Tables 1-9. These may be used for student classification, grading, or as a teaching aid to diagnose weaknesses in players or instruction.

Front Shot (Table 9.1)

1. Equipment
   a. One basketball
   b. One goal
2. Description
   a. Student shoots from a floor position on the free throw line extended, just outside and to the left of the restraining circle. Any type of shot is permissible.
   b. Fifteen trials are taken, five shots at a time.

[1] AAHPERD skills tests and accompanying tables in this chapter are reprinted by permission of the American Alliance for Health, Physical Education, Recreation and Dance, 1900 Association Drive, Reston, VA 22091, from *Basketball for Girls Skills Tests Manual*, 1966.

Table 9.1
AAHPERD Front Shot Test Scores
(In Points by Age)

Percentile	Male				Female			
	9-10	11-12	13-15	16-18	9-10	11-12	13-15	16-18
100	23	27	28	30	21	21	30	30
90	15	17	20	22	12	13	16	17
80	12	15	19	20	10	11	14	15
70	10	13	17	18	8	9	12	13
60	9	12	16	17	6	7	10	12
50	7	10	15	16	5	6	9	11
40	6	9	14	2	3	5	7	9
30	4	8	12	14	2	3	6	8
20	3	6	11	12	1	2	4	6
10	1	4	9	10	0	1	2	4
0	0	0	0	3	0	0	0	0

AAHPERD 1966.

c. After each series of five shots, student moves from the spot or allows another student to attempt five shots.

d. A practice shot is permitted.

3. Scoring

a. Two points are awarded for each basket made.

b. One point is awarded for shots that hit the rim but fail to enter the basket.

c. The maximum score is 30 points.

Side Shot (Table 9.2)

1. Equipment
   a. One basketball
   b. One goal
2. Description
   a. Student attempts ten shots from a line 20 ft to the right side of the basket.
   b. Student attempts ten shots from a line 20 ft to the left side of the basket.
   c. A practice shot is permitted.
3. Scoring
   a. Two points are scored for each goal made.
   b. One point is awarded each time a ball hits the rim without entering the basket.

Table 9.2
AAHPERD Side Shot Test Scores
(In Points by Age)

Percentile	Male				Female			
	10	11–12	13–15	16–18	10	11–12	13–15	16–18
100	27	31	34	36	25	26	30	32
90	14	18	23	25	13	14	18	20
80	11	15	20	22	11	12	16	17
70	8	13	18	20	8	9	14	15
60	6	11	16	18	6	7	12	13
50	5	9	15	17	4	5	11	12
40	3	7	14	16	3	4	9	10
30	2	6	12	14	1	2	7	8
20	1	4	10	12	0	1	5	6
10	0	3	6	9	0	0	2	3
0	0	0	2	2	0	0	0	0

AAHPERD 1966.

Foul Shot (Table 9.3)

1. Equipment
    a. One basketball
    b. One goal
2. Description
    a. Student attempts 20 shots in series of 5 at a time from behind the free throw line. Student must leave the free throw line after 5 shots are attempted, allowing another student to take a series of shots.
    b. A practice shot is permitted.
3. Scoring
    a. One point is scored for each goal.
    b. Maximum score is 20 points.

Under Basket Shot (Table 9.4)

1. Equipment
    a. One basketball
    b. One goal
    c. One stopwatch
2. Description
    a. Holding a ball, student assumes a position near the basket.

Table 9.3
AAHPERD Foul Shot Test Scores
(In Baskets by Age)

Percentile	Male				Female			
	10	11-12	13-15	16-18	10	11-12	13-15	16-18
100	13	12	20	20	20	20	20	20
90	5	8	11	13	5	6	7	9
80	4	6	10	11	4	5	6	7
70	3	5	8	9	3	4	4	6
60	2	4	7	8	2	3	3	5
50	2	4	6	8	1	2	3	4
40	1	3	5	7	1	2	2	4
30	1	2	4	5	0	1	2	3
20	0	2	5	4	0	1	2	2
10	0	1	3	3	0	0	1	2
0	0	0	0	0	0	0	0	0

AAHPERD 1966.

Table 9.4
AAHPERD Under Basket Shot Test Scores
(In Baskets by Age)

Percentile	Male				Female			
	9–10	11–12	13–15	16–18	9–10	11–12	13–15	16–18
100	14	23	25	34	15	15	17	20
90	9	11	15	18	7	8	9	11
80	7	9	14	16	5	6	8	9
70	6	8	12	15	5	6	7	8
60	5	7	11	16	4	5	6	7
50	5	6	10	13	4	4	6	6
40	4	5	8	11	3	4	5	5
30	3	5	8	10	3	3	4	4
20	3	4	7	9	2	3	4	4
10	2	3	7	7	1	2	3	3
0	0	1	1	1	0	0	1	1

AAHPERD 1966.

    b.   On the signal "go," student attempts rapid, continuous lay-up shots, trying to score as many baskets as possible in 30 sec.

    c.   Student continues shooting until "stop" signal is given.

    d.   A practice trial and two scoring trials are permitted.

3. Scoring

    a.   One point is scored for each basket made between the "go" and "stop" signals.

    b.   A ball in the air when the "stop" signal is given scores a point if the goal is made.

    c.   The better of the two scoring trials counts.

Speed Pass (Table 9.5)

1. Equipment

    a.   A level floor with a line drawn 9 ft from a smooth wall

    b.   One stopwatch

    c.   One basketball

2. Description

    a.   Student stands behind line, facing the wall.

    b.   On the signal "go," student repeatedly passes the ball against the wall as quickly as possible until ten passes have hit the wall. Any method of passing may be used, provided passes are made from a position behind the line.

    c.   A practice trial and two scoring trials are permitted.

Table 9.5
AAHPERD Speed Pass Test Scores
(In Seconds by Age)

Percentile	Male				Female			
	9–10	11–12	13–15	16–18	9–10	11–12	13–15	16–18
100	10.0	7.0	5.1	4.5	7.5	7.5	7.5	6.5
90	11.6	10.4	10.8	7.4	12.6	11.9	10.6	10.0
80	12.5	11.1	8.7	7.9	13.2	12.6	11.5	10.8
70	13.1	11.7	9.2	8.4	13.9	13.6	12.1	11.4
60	13.6	12.3	9.7	8.7	14.5	13.9	12.7	12.0
50	14.2	12.8	10.1	9.1	15.3	14.6	13.3	12.6
40	14.9	13.4	10.7	9.5	15.9	15.3	14.0	13.2
30	15.6	13.9	11.3	10.0	16.7	16.1	14.8	13.9
20	16.5	14.7	12.1	10.8	17.7	17.2	15.7	15.0
10	18.1	15.9	13.6	12.2	19.1	18.7	17.5	16.6
0	26.0	25.7	20.7	20.1	25.5	25.5	25.5	25.4

AAHPERD 1966.

3. Scoring
   a. Time in seconds is taken from the instant the first pass touches the wall until the tenth pass hits the wall.
   b. The better of the two scoring trials counts.

Jump and Reach (Table 9.6)

1. Equipment
   a. A level floor with a smooth wall
   b. One piece of chalk
   c. One tape measure or yardstick
2. Description
   a. Holding a piece of chalk, student stands with side to the wall.
   b. With feet flat on floor and body fully extended, student reaches upward as far as possible and makes a mark on the wall.
   c. From a crouched position, student then swings arms and jumps as high as possible with both feet, making a second mark on the wall.
   d. Distance between the marks is measured.
   e. A practice jump and two scoring trials are permitted.

Table 9.6
AAHPERD Jump and Reach Test Scores
(In Inches by Age)

Percentile	Male				Female			
	9-10	11-12	13-15	16-18	9-10	11-12	13-15	16-18
100	18	24	30	33	18	20	24	25
90	13	16	21	24	14	15	16	17
80	12	15	19	23	12	13	15	16
70	12	14	19	22	11	12	13	15
60	11	13	18	21	11	12	13	14
50	10	12	17	20	10	11	13	13
40	10	12	16	19	10	11	12	13
30	9	11	15	18	9	10	11	12
20	9	10	13	16	9	9	10	11
10	8	9	12	16	8	9	9	10
0	4	5	6	11	5	5	6	7

AAHPERD 1966.

3. Scoring
   a. The score is the distance to the nearest inch between the reaching and jumping marks.
   b. The better of the two trials counts.

Overarm Pass for Accuracy (Table 9.7)

1. Equipment
   a. One basketball
   b. One piece of chalk
   c. Measuring tape
   d. A circular wall target (Figure 9.1) with three concentric circles measuring 18, 38, and 58 in. in diameter (inner circle to outer). Lines are 1 in. wide; outer circle is 3 ft from the floor.
2. Description
   a. Holding a basketball, student stands behind a line parallel to and 35 ft from the wall target.
   b. Using an overarm throw with one step permitted, student makes ten passes at the target from behind the throwing line.
   c. Balls hitting on lines count the higher value.
   d. One practice pass is permitted.

Table 9.7
AAHPERD Overarm Pass for Accuracy Test Scores
(In Points by Age)

Percentile	Male				Female			
	9–10	11–12	13–15	16–18	9–10	11–12	13–15	16–18
100	18	27	29	31	27	28	30	30
90	13	17	21	23	22	23	24	25
80	10	14	19	21	19	20	22	23
70	7	13	18	19	17	18	21	22
60	6	11	16	17	14	16	19	21
50	4	9	15	16	12	14	18	19
40	2	8	14	15	10	12	16	17
30	1	6	12	13	7	10	15	15
20	0	4	10	11	4	7	12	13
10	0	2	8	9	0	2	8	9
0	0	0	0	1	0	0	0	0

AAHPERD 1966.

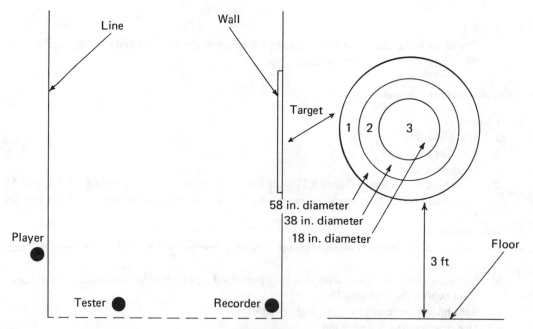

Figure 9.1
Overarm pass target

3. Scoring
    a. For each pass thrown, 3 points are scored for hits in the inner circle, 2 points for hits in the middle circle, and 1 point for hits in the outer circle.
    b. Points are totaled, with maximum score of 30 points.

Push Pass for Accuracy (Table 9.8)

1. Equipment
    a. One basketball
    b. One piece of chalk
    c. Measuring tape
    d. Wall with marked target as described in overarm pass for accuracy
2. Description
    a. Holding a ball, student stands behind a restraining line 25 ft from and parallel to the wall.
    b. Using a two-hand push pass, student aims for the center of the target and attempts ten passes against the wall.
    c. One practice pass is permitted.
3. Scoring is the same as in overarm pass for accuracy.

Table 9.8
AAHPERD Push Pass for Accuracy Test Scores
(In Points by Age)

Percentile	Male				Female			
	9–10	11–12	13–15	16–18	9–10	11–12	13–15	16–18
100	18	29	29	30	18	20	24	25
90	14	19	24	27	14	15	16	17
80	12	14	21	26	12	13	15	16
70	11	11	20	25	11	12	14	15
60	11	9	18	24	11	12	13	14
50	10	8	18	23	10	11	13	13
40	10	5	15	21	10	11	12	13
30	9	3	13	20	9	9	11	12
20	9	2	11	18	9	9	10	11
10	8	1	7	15	8	9	9	10
0	5	0	2	5	5	5	6	7

AAHPERD 1966.

Dribble (Table 9.9)

1. Equipment
   a. One basketball
   b. Six chairs arranged in single file as shown in Figure 9.2
2. Description
   a. On the signal "go," student begins dribbling at the starting line and weaves in and out around the six chairs.
   b. After weaving around the sixth chair, student continues the pattern in reverse order and crosses the starting line.
   c. At least one dribble must be made as each chair is passed.
   d. One practice trial and two scoring trials are permitted.
3. Scoring
   a. Time is recorded in seconds and tenths, beginning at the signal "go" and stopping as student crosses the starting line on return.
   b. Score is the better of the two trials.

Because the administration of all nine tests is time-consuming, the teacher or coach may prefer to administer a select few that are most appropriate for the situation. Hopkins (1979) found that two of the performance tests—the under basket shot and the dribble—provided the same discriminating

Table 9.9
AAHPERD Dribbling Test Scores
(In Seconds by Age)

	Male				Female			
Percentile	**9-10**	**11-12**	**13-15**	**16-18**	**9-10**	**11-12**	**13-15**	**16-18**
100	12.0	8.5	6.2	5.5	27	28	30	30
90	13.7	11.5	10.1	9.7	22	23	24	25
80	14.6	12.7	10.8	10.3	19	20	22	23
70	15.1	13.3	11.3	10.8	17	18	21	22
60	15.5	13.8	11.9	11.3	14	16	19	21
50	16.0	14.4	12.4	11.8	12	14	18	19
40	16.5	15.0	13.0	12.1	10	12	16	17
30	17.2	15.7	14.0	12.8	7	10	15	15
20	18.0	16.5	14.3	13.4	4	7	12	13
10	19.4	18.0	15.6	14.7	0	2	8	9
0	26.0	26.5	22.3	21.6	0	0	0	0

AAHPERD 1966.

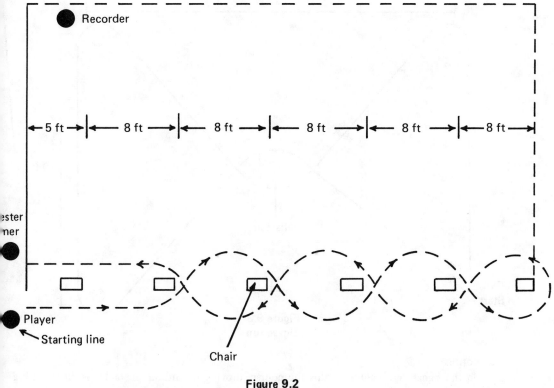

Figure 9.2
Dribble test layout

information as all nine items when administered to a group of 60 high school girls. Although the two tests cannot provide overall evaluations of skill, they can offer a quick and objective preliminary assessment.

In another study, Hopkins (1979) recommends using six test items to measure skill and distinguish between potentially successful and unsuccessful basketball players—speed pass, zigzag run, free jump, side step, front shot, and zigzag dribble. The AAHPERD speed pass, zigzag dribble, and front shot tests have been described previously. The other suggested tests are described below.

Other Recommended Tests

Zigzag Run (Figure 9.3)

1. Facilities and equipment
   a. Measured test course consisting of five obstacles
   b. Five cones
   c. One stopwatch

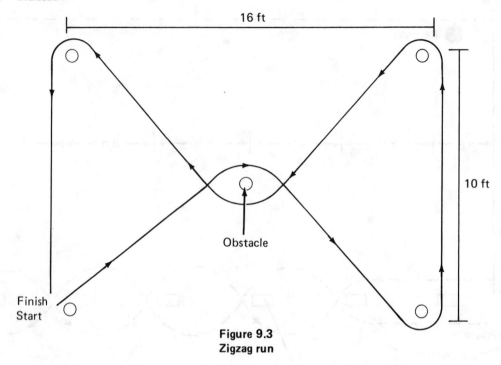

Figure 9.3
Zigzag run

2. Description
   a. On the signal "go," student runs the course, moving around the obstacles as shown in Figure 9.3.
   b. Student crosses the starting point at full speed.
   c. Two trials are permitted.
3. Scoring
   a. The score is time in seconds to the nearest tenth needed to complete the course.
   b. The better of the two trials counts.

Free Jump

The free jump is the same as the AAHPERD jump and reach test, except that participants are allowed to move one foot before takeoff. This alteration is designed to offer a better simulation of the jumping movement (e.g., for jump balls, jump shots, taking rebounds) than does the AAHPERD test.

Side Step

1. Facilities and equipment
   a. Two lines on the floor 12 ft apart
   b. One stopwatch
2. Description
   a. Student stands between the two lines, with one foot touching a sideline.
   b. On the signal "go," student moves sideward with a side step, leading with the foot nearest the line being approached, and continues sidestepping until the foot has touched or crossed the line.

3.   Scoring
    a.   One point is scored each time a line is touched.

Several other skill tests may help an instructor to measure a player's skill in shooting, dribbling, and taking rebounds.

Twelve-Foot Shooting (Cunningham 1965) (Figure 9.4)

1.   Facilities and equipment
    a.   Two basketballs
    b.   One basket
    c.   Three areas marked on the floor; boundaries are free throw lane lines and a semicircle with a 12-ft radius (the center being directly under the attachment of the basket to the backboard). As shown in Figure 9.4, Area I is outside the semicircle to the left of the free throw lane, Area II is outside the semicircle and between the free throw lane lines, and Area III is opposite Area I to the right of the free throw lane.
2.   Description
    a.   Standing anywhere in Area I, the student shoots ten balls. As soon as one ball is shot, a rebounder passes a second ball to the shooter.
    b.   After each shot, the student must move one step to the right or left.
    c.   Ten shots are taken from Area II and ten from Area III.
3.   Scoring
    a.   Three points are scored for each basket made, and 1 point for a rim shot.
    b.   Points are totaled from shots in all three areas.

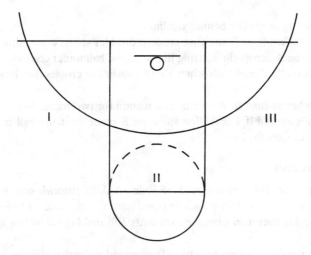

Figure 9.4
Twelve-foot shooting test

Ten-Second Rebound Test

The 10-sec rebound test measures ability to take a rebound.

1. Equipment
   a. One stopwatch
   b. One basketball per station
   c. One backboard per station
2. Description
   a. Students line up single file at each station.
   b. On the signal "ready-go," the first student tosses a ball at the backboard and takes a rebound.
   c. Student continues tossing and rebounding ball for 10 sec. Consecutively tapping the ball is recommended.
   d. Other students at the station count rebounds or taps, and record them.
3. Scoring
   a. Score is total rebounds for two trials.
   b. If a ball has been tossed or tapped and time expires before it reaches the backboard, the rebound counts.

Dribble and Shoot Test

The dribble and shoot test measures ability to dribble rapidly, control the ball, and shoot.

1. Equipment
   a. One stopwatch
   b. Two basketballs
   c. One side basket with 55 ft of floor space
2. Description
   a. Students line up single file behind sideline.
   b. On the signal "ready-go," the first student dribbles across court, shoots until shot is made, and dribbles back across the starting line with the ball under control.
   c. Time begins on "go" and ends when a foot touches or crosses the finish line.
3. Scoring
   a. Score is the better time to the tenth of a second for two trials.
   b. A trial is discounted if a dribbling violation is made or if the ball is not under control as the student crosses the line.

Rating Scales and Checklists

In addition to the objective measurement of isolated skills through skill tests, a comprehensive analysis of a student's ability includes assessing performance in game situations. Rating scales and checklists can aid the instructor in observing students and making subjective appraisals of skill and behavior.

Checklists itemize specific components of offensive and defensive abilities appropriate for a particular level of skill. Adjacent to the listing are spaces in which to indicate the presence or absence of each component. Checklists may also take a form of incidence charts, on which each occurrence of a particular action is indicated by a check mark.

Rating scales not only indicate the presence of a skill but also allow the observer to designate the level of proficiency with which the skill is executed. A sample rating scale for beginning level individual players is shown in Figure 9.5.

Skill Components	5	4	3	2	1
Passing					
Accuracy					
Crispness (wrist snap)					
Deception					
Fingertip control					
Receiving					
Watching ball					
Relaxing fingers					
Hands above waist					
Moving or cutting to meet the pass					
Dribbling					
Fingertip control					
Head up					
Change of pace and direction					
Protecting ball					
Speed					
Shooting					
Quickness					
Eye on target					
Balance with shoulders squared					
Follow through					
Softness of shot					
Shot selected					

Directions: Rate student on each of the skill components on a scale of 5 to 1: 5 = exceptional ability for the age, level, and sex; 4 = above-average ability; 3 = average ability; 2 = below-average ability; 1 = inferior ability.

Figure 9.5
Sample rating scale for beginning level individual players

NAME OF TEAM _____

NAMES OF PLAYERS	NUMBERS	TIMES IN GAME	GOALS		INDIVIDUAL FOULS	GOALS		SUMMARY			
			1st QUARTER	2nd QUARTER	1 2 3 4 5	3rd QUARTER	4th QUARTER	FG	FT	F	PTS
					1 2 3 4 5						
					1 2 3 4 5						
					1 2 3 4 5						
					1 2 3 4 5						
					1 2 3 4 5						
					1 2 3 4 5						
					1 2 3 4 5						
					1 2 3 4 5						
					1 2 3 4 5						
					1 2 3 4 5						
					1 2 3 4 5						
					1 2 3 4 5						
					1 2 3 4 5						
					1 2 3 4 5						
					1 2 3 4 5						
					1 2 3 4 5						
					1 2 3 4 5						
					1 2 3 4 5			TOTALS			

TEAM TIME-OUTS
1	2	3	4	5

TEAM FOULS
1	2	3	4	5

WON BY _____
SCORE _____

DATE _____
PLACE _____

RUNNING SCORE

1	2	3	4	5	6	7	8	9	10	11	12	13	14	15	16	17	18	19	20	21	22	23	24	25	26	27	28	29	30	31	32	33	34	35	36	37	38	39	40
41	42	43	44	45	46	47	48	49	50	51	52	53	54	55	56	57	58	59	60	61	62	63	64	65	66	67	68	69	70	71	72	73	74	75	76	77	78	79	80

Figure 9.6
Score sheet summary

Charting Statistics

Summarized game statistics can provide vital information for analyzing individual and team performance. Because this evaluative technique can reveal strengths and weaknesses of instruction, it can help teachers structure future classes or team practices. Charts can be predrawn; student leaders, assistants, or nonparticipating students can be trained to record data. The score sheet summary provides information on field goals attempted and made, free throws attempted and made, fouls, and total points scored by individuals and teams (Figure 9.6).

The following charts may be used to record further information for the analysis of skills. In interpreting frequency statistics, the teacher or coach should consider the amount of playing time each individual has had.

Shot Chart (Figure 9.7)

Attempted shots are designated on the court diagram by recording the pinnie or uniform number of the player at the approximate location on the court. If the shot is successful, a circle is drawn around the number. If fouled in the act of shooting, the player receives an F beside his or her number. A shot chart may be kept for each period or half of the game. Shots for both teams may be recorded on the same sheet. Team totals for shots attempted as well as the percentage of shots made may be recorded at the bottom of the chart.

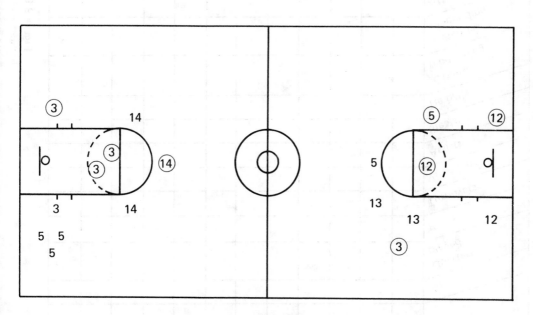

Figure 9.7
Shot chart

Figure 9.8
Incidence chart

Name	No.	Quarters played	Fouls	Turnovers	Violations	Assists	Steals	Tie balls	Offensive rebounding	Defensive rebounding	Field goals					Free throws					Points by Quarters					Total points
											Attempted	Made	Missed	%	Attempted	Made	Missed	%	1	2	3	4	Ex		
Team totals																									

Incidence Chart (Figure 9.8)

The number of assists, rebounds, turnovers, fouls, violations, tie balls, and steals may be indicated on an incidence chart.

Jump Ball Chart

The jump ball chart tallies the number of jump balls lost and retained as well as scores made directly from the tap by each team for each period.

Error Chart (Figure 9.9)

The error chart indicates the number of the player and type of turnover made. A large number of turnovers indicates a breakdown in teamwork or faulty individual performance or both.

Composite game statistics can be converted into player ratings to determine the playing value of each team member. One conversion method awards the following values to each statistic (Sands 1973): +1 point for each field goal, free throw, rebound, assist, defensive play (steal or steal caused); -1 point for turnovers.

Standards are established for free throw and field goal accuracy. The difference between the expected standard percentages and the individual's accuracy percentages, for both free throws and field goals, is determined. Each difference is multiplied by the player's number of field goals or number of free throws. This figure is subtracted from the player's field goals or free throws if the player's percentage is lower than the established percentage. For example, if the player's 80 successful field goals yield a percentage that is 5 percent below the field goal standard, multiply 0.05 times 80 to equal 4.0, and subtract the 4.0 from 80 to give a rating of 76. If the percentage is higher than the standard, the figure is added to the player's number of field goals or free throws. This gives the adjusted field goals and adjusted free throws for the formula

$$\text{Rating} = \frac{\text{adjusted field goals} + \text{adjusted free throws} + \text{rebounds} + \text{assists} + \text{defensive plays} - \text{turnovers}}{\text{playing time}}$$

Individual ratings may then be compared with those of other team members.

COGNITIVE ASSESSMENT

Written quiz and examination questions should reflect the information given students through class discussions, handouts, and reading assignments on game rules, strategies, techniques, and etiquette. Test and measurement textbooks offer the novice teacher guidelines in preparing explicit true-false, multiple-choice, matching, and essay questions. In devising or selecting tests, instructors should consider the clarity and grading time of an examination, as well as the extent to which it can be used to make meaningful discriminations among students. Table 9.10 shows suggested content of written assessments for beginning and advanced classes.

Other instruments or techniques found useful in the periodic assessment of learning include crossword or scramble word puzzles (using basketball terminology), verbal question-and-answer sessions, college bowl competition, worksheets, and outside assignments such as recording statistics for a game attended.

Name	Number	Pass		Violation	Offensive foul	Tied ball	Total
Team total							

Possession lost

Figure 9.9
Error chart

Table 9.10
Suggested Content of
Written Assessments for Beginning and Advanced Classes

Beginning	Advanced
History and values of game	New terminology
Safety	Situations for rules application
Basic terminology	Intermediate skill techniques
Rules	Passing
Playing court	Hook
Players and substitutions	One-hand bounce
Jump balls	Overarm
Out of bounds	Behind the back
Free throws	Lob
Field goals	On run
Violations and penalties	Shooting
General fouls and penalties	Lay-ups
Beginning skill techniques	Either hand
Passing	Reverse
Underhand	Jump
Chest	Hook
Bounce	Dribbling
Overarm	Speed dribble
Stationary and moving	Control dribble
receivers	Behind the back
Receiving	Crossover
Footwork and pivoting	Reverse
Shooting	Rebounding
Lay-ups	Defensive
Set shots	Offensive
Free throws	Defensive techniques
Dribbling	Switching
Dominant hand	Trapping
Nondominant hand	Baseline
Guarding	Strategy
Rebounding	Defensive
Player-to-player strategy	Zone defense
Defensive	Against fast break
Offensive	Pressure
Screening	Team defenses
Cutting	Offensive
Give and go	Against player-to-player defense
Split the post	Against zone defense
	Fast break
	Breaking the press
	Officiating
	Scorekeeping

AFFECTIVE ASSESSMENT

Intangible personal qualities such as attitude, values, cooperation, and emotional maturity are difficult to measure precisely. Physical educators and coaches recognize these characteristics, which are associated with the affective domain, as important factors in the total development of the individual. Sociometric ratings as well as scales assessing attitude, leadership, and sportsmanship have been developed to assist in the evaluation process. One scale we recommend—the Kenyon Attitude Scale for college students—was designed to measure six separate dimensions of attitude toward physical activity: social experience, health and fitness, pursuit of vertigo, aesthetic experience, catharsis, and ascetic experience (Kenyon 1968). The multidimensional measurement this scale provides is more reliable and valid than the single general factor that other attitude scales measure.

Another frequently used scale that is applicable to basketball players is the Wear Attitude Scale. This scale elicits responses to statements regarding the physiological-physical, mental-emotional, social, and general values of physical education (Baumgartner and Jackson 1975).

Results of these assessments may indicate a player's congruence or incongruence with the philosophy of the coach or team. They also may help teachers to understand their students and arrive at effective motivational techniques.

Barrow and McGee (1971) designed a scale to measure sportsmanship attitudes of high school students. The total questionnaire consists of 48 statements relating to five specific sports and a general sports category. Students are asked to judge the positive and negative behavior described in the statements. The portion of the scale presented in Figure 9.10 includes sample statements about attitudes related to basketball.

Instructions: Place in the space beside each statement the number of the response that describes the way you think about that statement (5 = strongly agree, 4 = agree, 3 = undecided, 2 = disagree, 1 = strongly disagree).

_____ A basketball player told the official he/she touched the ball as it went out-of-bounds.

_____ A basketball player moved quietly toward the bench when he/she fouled out of the game.

_____ A member of the home basketball team told the official that the shot that apparently won the game was released after the buzzer sounded.

_____ Following a very close game, opposing teams shook hands as they left the court.

_____ A basketball player admitted touching the rim of the basket in a controversial goal-tending call.

_____ A guard continually tagged his/her opponent in order to distract him/her.

Figure 9.10
Sportsmanship attitude questionnaire (modified from Barrow and McGee 1979)

Another instrument applicable to high school or college athletes is the Athletic Motivation Inventory (Ogilvie and Tutko 1972), which measures the psychological traits related to high athletic achievement and offers coaches insight in assisting new athletes. It may also provide the student athlete with information that can be used for self-improvement.

Other inventories that offer insight into the personalities of athletes include the Edwards Personal Preference Schedule (Edwards 1953), which assesses the relative strength of 15 needs by determining how an individual would react under ordinary conditions of life. The Myers-Briggs Type Indicator (Myers 1970) examines four basic preferences that relate to the way an individual perceives the environment and determines whether he or she will derive personal satisfaction from daily work and selected activities.

Sociometric tests ask group members to describe their thoughts about their fellow teammates or classmates. The tests are designed to assess each player's desirability and acceptance or rejection as a team member. This information may assist in identifying potential team leaders, placing students on teams, and determining each student's contribution to the team effort.

PROJECTS FOR PROSPECTIVE TEACHERS

1. Administer, or assist in administering, one of the basketball performance tests to a group of students. Help the students compare their scores to available norms.
2. Request data on a particular skill test from a teacher who has administered the test to his or her classes. Establish a set of norms based on the data. Compare averages taken from various classes.
3. Develop a written basketball test based on cognitive objectives appropriate to a high school class. The test should consist of 25 true-false and 25 multiple-choice questions. Administer the test to ten of your classmates as a pilot study. Perform and review an item analysis on each question to determine possible ambiguity.
4. Self-administer a leadership inventory. What did you learn about yourself? How might what you learned affect your style of teaching?

References

Barrow, H. M., and McGee, R. *A Practical Approach to Measurement in Physical Education.* 2nd ed. Philadelphia: Lea and Febiger, 1971.

Baumgartner, T., and Jackson, A. *Measurement for Evaluation in Physical Education.* Boston: Houghton Mifflin Co., 1975.

Cunningham, P. "Basketball Skill Tests for High School Girls." *Basketball Guide.* Reston, Va.: AAHPERD, 1965.

Edwards, A. *Edwards Personal Preference Schedule.* New York: Psychological Corporation, 1953.

Hopkins, D. "Using Skill Tests to Identify Successful and Unsuccessful Basketball Performers." *Research Quarterly* 50(1979):381-387.

Kenyon, G. S. "Sex Scales for Assessing Attitude Toward Physical Activity." *Research Quarterly* 39(1968):556-574.

McMahan, R. "The Development of an Instrument for Assessing Sportsmanship Attitudes." Ph.D. dissertation, University of Tennessee, Knoxville, 1978.

Myers, I. *Introduction to Type.* Swarthmore, Pa.: Isabel Myers, 1970.

Ogilvie, B., and Tutko, T. *Athletic Motivation Inventory.* San Jose, Calif.: Institute of Athletic Motivation, 1972.

Sands, Gary. "Individually Rating Basketball Players." *Athletic Journal* 53(1973):53.

10

Coaching Tips

Coaching can be an especially rewarding teaching situation, because the coach is working with a relatively small, select group. As is the case with any special group, however, a special kind of person is required to do the job properly. To be a good coach, one must first be a good teacher.

Hundreds of books deal with the techniques of coaching basketball, and the subject certainly cannot be completely covered in one chapter of this text. Consequently, we will present a few general observations that may be of some benefit to the prospective coach.

Preseason Planning (Reynolds 1969)

Before the season begins, the coach must spend many hours taking care of matters such as game schedules, contracts, officials, budgeting, transportation, medical examinations, practice schedules, facilities, and equipment. The regulating association's handbook and the director of athletics can help the new coach become familiar with procedures and people to contact.

Although the situation varies from school to school scheduling is usually left to the coach, subject to the approval of the director of athletics or the principal or both. Scheduling often takes place during the previous season when the coach is in contact with other coaches. Many conferences have a master schedule for all conference games; in high schools, the state athletic association sets the dates for beginning the season and for the play-offs at the end of the season. The state association also determines the number of games that may be played.

Contracts

A written contract should cover all games between the schools involved. This contract should state clearly all conditions of the athletic contest, including date, time, place, officials to be used, monetary considerations, and any other appropriate information. All contracts should provide a place for the principal of each school to sign. Game contracts should be in duplicate so that each school has its own copy.

Officials

In most of the better-organized leagues or conferences, a person or agency schedules officials. Although this method is preferable, the coach is sometimes responsible for securing officials. In this case, the coach should avoid officials with close ties to the school and those who have a reputation for calling in favor of the home team. Generally, the visiting team should be given the opportunity to agree on the officials.

All officials whom the coach secures should be under contract for each game. This contract should include such information as time, date, place, schools involved, officials' fee, and time that the officials are to be at the game site. If officials are assigned by a booking agency, a second contract is not always necessary; however, officials should receive a notification card a few days before the game reminding them of game time, date, and place.

Budgeting

Each year just after completing the basketball season, the coach needs to prepare a budget for the following year. The budget request should include all anticipated expenditures for uniforms and equipment, officials, travel, facilities, utilities, laundry service, training room supplies, and maintenance.

All anticipated receipts from ticket sales, donations, fund raising, school allocations, and guarantees should also be listed. If the receipts are equal to, or greater than, the estimated expenditures, the budget request is more likely to be approved. Once the budget is prepared, it should be submitted to the director of athletics for approval.

Selecting and Purchasing Equipment

Most schools have some policy regarding purchasing supplies and equipment. The new coach should become familiar with this policy immediately. Usually, the director of athletics should approve all purchases.

In the selection of equipment and supplies, experience shows that the purchase of quality goods pays. Doing business with local dealers is good public relations if they can offer equal value and service. Always purchase from a reputable dealer.

Travel

The transportation of players is one of the problem areas of interscholastic athletics. Whenever possible, school-owned vehicles or a commercial carrier should be used. Use of personal vehicles to transport players may cause an insurance or liability problem and is not recommended.

Public Relations

Public relations is an essential part of the duties of every successful coach. In most communities, the high school basketball coach is an important person; establishing good public relations generally results in solid community support.

The coach should accept as many speaking engagements as possible. The people in the community want to hear about basketball, so the coach should stay on that subject and keep the talks brief. Such engagements offer opportunities for initiating booster or support groups for the program.

Facilities and Equipment

Facilities and equipment should be kept as clean and bright as possible. Their appearance is an important factor in any successful basketball program.

One way to improve and maintain facilities is for the coaching staff and prospective players to have a clean-up session on a Saturday morning before the practice season starts. Some parents or supporters are usually glad to help. Athletes who take part in cleaning and brightening the facilities strive to maintain them in that condition; the work becomes a source of pride.

The coach is responsible to see that all practice and game equipment is clean and in proper condition for use. Providing the team with the best equipment possible is important. A team with good, well-cared-for equipment seems to take more pride in what they do. Generally, the coach selects one or more equipment managers to help care for the equipment.

Preseason Workouts

Any preseason practice schedule depends on several factors, such as state or local regulations, other fall sports, and in many cases, other extracurricular and work obligations of the students. Regardless of the restraints that may be imposed, the preseason is an excellent time to initiate a sound conditioning program and work on individual skills. One successful basketball coach encouraged all prospective players who were not involved in another fall sport to run with the cross-country team. Those athletes who did so had little difficulty adjusting to conditioning drills when basketball practice started. Other coaches use a weight training program during the preseason. Although prospective players cannot be required to participate in preseason programs, they should be encouraged to do so.

Prepractice Meeting

A meeting of all prospective team members a day or so before practice starts is always a good idea. At this meeting, the coach should inform the prospects of eligibility rules, methods of selecting team members, practice times, and conditioning and training rules. Each prospect should be clear about what to expect of the coach, and what the coach expects of each prospect.

Each of these items must be explained thoroughly, and each prospective player must have an opportunity to pose questions about any item not fully understood.

Selecting the Squad

Because basketball is so popular, many more people are likely to try out than can be used on the team. The coach's most difficult task is to reduce the squad to the appropriate size. Each prospective player should be given fair opportunity to demonstrate ability. During the first week of practice, the coach should eliminate those players who are unable to play at the required level. Many such students leave voluntarily when they see they cannot compete.

During the second week of practice, the remaining players should be classified according to the positions they are likely to play. Execution of fundamental skills should be paramount in assessing each player's ability. A series of scrimmages should be held during the week to allow each player to play on teams composed of different members.

In addition to skill, other factors should be considered in making the final squad cuts. Grade level is a factor (e.g., a sophomore should be given preference over a senior). Eligibility should be checked. Do not waste time on an ineligible player. Because of the nature of the game, a positive, assertive attitude and the desire to be a team player are qualities that should be sought in each prospect. Have a conference with each player who fails to demonstrate a constructive attitude. Sometimes basketball can be the one thing to help a student reevaluate his or her life-style, and the coach can be influential in enabling that student to make a turnaround. Finally, the head coach should have a personal talk with each prospect being cut and inform the prospect that he or she is not ready to play with the team. Offer these students suggestions for improving their game and invite them to try out again the following year. Answer any questions the prospect may have, and allow those who believe that they have not had an adequate opportunity to try another time. No prospect should ever feel that he or she has been discriminated against.

Student Managers

Student managers are an important part of any athletic program and should be selected with care. Coaches often find that prospective athletes who cannot make the squad are anxious to be a part of the program. Such students usually make excellent managers; they can assist in activities such as keeping records, managing equipment, and hosting officials and visiting teams.

In-Season Practice

To be efficient, a practice session must be organized. The successful coach knows what must be worked on each day, and allots sufficient time to each aspect of practice.

Although practice sessions vary slightly in length, they generally should run from 1½ to a maximum of 2 hr. The last practice before a game is usually somewhat shorter or less strenuous than others. As the season progresses, giving the squad a day off is sometimes advantageous; this is particularly effective as positive reinforcement after a big win.

Fundamentals should be a basic part of the practice session every day (Table 10.1). Often, the first two weeks of practice are used to install the offensive system. Once the players know the offense and have confidence in it, more time should be spent on defense. After the first game and for the remainder of the season, 2 min should be spent on defense for every minute spent on offense.

Summary

Listing all the characteristics of the good coach is impossible. The good coach is one who does more than just direct practice sessions and game situations. To meet the needs of the young athlete, the good coach must at times assume many roles, as a substitute mother or father, sister or brother,

Table 10.1
Sample Practice Schedule

Time	Activity
3:30-3:40	Free throws
3:40-3:55	Game shots, individual work
3:55-4:10	Fundamental drills
4:10-4:30	Offensive patterns
4:30-5:10	Team defense
5:10-5:20	Special situations
5:20-5:25	Spot shooting
5:25-5:30	Free throws

judge or jury, clergyperson, counselor, confidante, or friend. When a prospective coach takes on the job of coach, he or she inherits tremendous responsibilities that should be taken seriously.

PROJECTS FOR PROSPECTIVE COACHES

1. Visit at least two high schools and observe a practice session in each. Compare the practice sessions, listing the similarities and differences.
2. Observe a basketball game and compare the coaching techniques that each coach uses.
3. Most coaches take the floor 30 min before game time for warm-ups. Design a 30-min pregame warm-up period.

Reference

Reynolds, H. M. "A Study to Develop Guidelines for Selected Administrative Practices of the Directors of Athletics in Kentucky High Schools." Ph.D. dissertation, University of Kentucky, Lexington, 1969.

Glossary

Assist   Credit awarded a player for a pass that results in an immediate score.

Backcourt   The half of the court containing the opponents' basket.

Back door (reverse) cut   The sudden movement of an offensive player behind the defender toward the basket.

Block out   Defensive technique used to prevent an offensive player from gaining a good rebounding position.

Double team   Two defensive team members guarding an offensive opponent.

Drive   A sudden move into an open space by an offensive player dribbling the ball.

Feint   A fake movement with the ball or body that is intended to deceive the opponent.

Front   Defensive technique in which a defender stands between the opponent and the ball.

Front court   The half of the court containing the team's own basket.

Give and go   Offensive play in which a player passes to a teammate and cuts into a space for a return pass.

High post   A pivot player's position at or around the free throw line.

Low post   A pivot player's position in the free throw lane or outside the lane within 10 ft of the basket.

Outlet pass   Initial pass after a rebound, generally directed toward the sideline.

Overloading a zone   Offensive tactic designed to position more offensive than defensive players in an area.

Overplay   Defensive technique in which the defender plays slightly to one side of the opponent instead of directly between the player and the basket.

Pick   Offensive technique in which a player with the ball drives around a stationary teammate to lose a guard.

Pivot or post player   An offensive player who maneuvers close to the basket.

Player-to-player defense   Each defensive player guards an assigned opponent.

Press   Pressure defense designed to force the opponents into making errors.

Roll   Offensive technique in which a player without the ball cuts for the basket after setting a screen.

Turnover Offensive team loses possession of the ball before attempting a shot. May be the result of a violation, an interception, or allowing the ball to go out-of-bounds.

Weak side Side of an offensive alignment that has the fewest players.

Wing Offensive player who plays near the sideline of the court opposite the free throw line.

Zone defense Defensive alignment in which players assume a position in relation to the ball and are responsible for particular areas on the court rather than specific opponents.

Annotated Bibliography

GENERAL

AAHPERD. *Basketball Skills Tests Manual for Girls.* Reston, Va.: AAHPERD, 1966.
AAHPERD. *Basketball Skills Tests Manual for Boys.* Reston, Va.: AAHPERD, 1966.
   Describe performance tests designed to assess mastery of basic basketball skills. Administrative procedures and national norms on students aged 10 through 18 are provided to assist the physical educator.

AAHPERD. *Planning Facilities for Athletics, Physical Education, and Recreation,* Reston, Va.: AAHPERD, 1974.
   Offers a section on planning and constructing basketball facilities.

Anderson, M.; Anderson, E.; Anderson, M.; and LaBerge, J. *Play With a Purpose.* New York: Harper and Row, 1966.
   An excellent source of lead-up games for a variety of activities.

Barnes, M. *Women's Basketball.* Boston: Allyn and Bacon, 1973.
   An excellent guidebook of tips, techniques, and strategies for the teacher, coach, and player. Applicable drills and diagrams accompany descriptions of offensive and defensive tactics.

Bee, C. *Drills and Fundamentals.* New York: A. S. Barnes and Co., 1942.
   Contains ageless drills to develop fundamental skills.

Bell, M. *Women's Basketball.* 2nd ed. Dubuque, Ia.: William C. Brown Co., 1975.
   Contains basic instructional material for teaching beginning skills and team offensive and defensive strategy.

Bunn, J. *Basketball Techniques and Team Play.* Englewood Cliffs, N.J.: Prentice-Hall, Inc., 1965.

Cooper, J., and Siedentop, D. *The Theory and Science of Basketball.* Philadelphia: Lea and Febiger, 1975.
   Contains basic principles for developing offensive and defensive systems; applies a scientific analysis of human movement to the coaching of basketball.

Cousy, B., and Power, F. G., Jr. *Basketball Concepts and Techniques.* Boston: Allyn and Bacon, 1970.
   "Mr. Basketball" of the Boston Celtics and a highly successful high school coach combine talents to present an informative book on the techniques of playing and coaching basketball. Key features include defensive tactics and tips for executing the fast break.

Ebert, F., and Cheatum, B. *Basketball*. Philadelphia: W. B. Saunders Co., 1977.
Uses approximately 300 illustrations and 200 drills to supplement explanations on techniques and strategies of the game.

Lindeburg, F. A. *How to Play and Teach Basketball*. 2nd ed. New York: Association Press, 1967.
Revised edition contains descriptions of various team offenses and defenses.

McGuire, F. *Defensive Basketball*. Englewood Cliffs, N.J.: Prentice-Hall, Inc., 1959.
A defense-minded coach offers his theories and thoughts on developing good team defense. Game organization and scouting tips are included.

McGuire, F. *Offensive Basketball*. Englewood Cliffs, N.J.: Prentice-Hall, Inc., 1958.
This outstanding coach shares his philosophy and views on establishing team offense.

Moore, B., and White, J. *Basketball: Theory and Practice*. Dubuque, Ia.: William C. Brown Co., 1980.
A theoretical, philosophical, and practical guide for teachers and coaches. Contains excellent tips from a successful coach on designing offenses, defenses, and plays for special situations.

National Federation of State High School Athletic Associations. *1981 Basketball Rule Book*. Elgin, Ill.: NFSHSAA, 1980.
The official rule book governing high school play. Contains a section on clarification and the application of various rules to specific situations.

Neal, P. *Basketball Techniques for Women*. New York: Ronald Press Co., 1966.
This outstanding player and teacher offers detailed insight into the training of the female basketball player. Contains sound information on conditioning, fundamentals, and game strategy.

Neal, P., and Tutko, T. *Coaching Girls and Women*. Boston: Allyn and Bacon, 1975.
A contemporary approach to coaching the skilled female athlete in competition, including psychological and physical aspects.

Richards, J. *Treasury of Basketball Drills From Top Coaches*. West Nyack, N.Y.: Parker Publishing Co., 1971.
Useful collection of basketball drills for coaches of all levels of experience.

Rupp, A. *Adolph Rupp's Basketball Guidebook*. New York: McGraw-Hill, 1967.
The "baron of basketball" describes fundamental techniques and plays appropriate for instructing players 9 years old and up.

Rupp, A. *Rupp's Championship Basketball*. Englewood Cliffs, N.J.: Prentice-Hall, Inc., 1957.
A basketball classic for coaches and scholars of the game.

Thompson, P.; Thompson, B.; Thompson, K.; and Van Whitley, A. "Mixed Murals." *JOHPERD* 45(1974):79.
Suggests game adaptations for coeducational play.

Thomson, J. "Basketball for Large Groups." *Division for Girls' and Women's Sports Basketball Guide*. Reston, Va.: AAHPERD, 1964.
Includes organizational techniques for teaching basketball to classes of more than 35 students.

Wooden, J. *Practical Modern Basketball*. New York: Ronald Press Co., 1966.
One of the winningest coaches in the game offers his suggestions on coaching, individual and team offense, and defenses and strategy for specific situations.

PERIODICALS

Athletic Journal (1719 Howard St., Evanston, IL 60202)
A monthly publication containing articles and features on coaching strategies, drills, and techniques for seasonal sports.

Coach and Athlete (200 S. Hull St., Montgomery, AL 36104)
A bimonthly official publication of numerous associations for coaches, trainers, and officials that includes technical articles and feature material for fans.

Coaching Clinic (P.O. Box 14, West Nyack, NY 10094)
A monthly publication featuring articles on coaching various sports by successful high school and college coaches throughout the country.

Scholastic Coach (50 W. 44th St., New York, NY 10036)
A monthly magazine for coaches, athletic directors, trainers, physical educators, and officials. Contains technical and administrative information for men's and women's sports programs.

SPECIAL ANNUAL PUBLICATIONS

AAHPERD. *Basketball Guide.* Reston, Va.: AAHPERD.
Contains the official rules for girls' and women's basketball, regulations for competition, and officiating information.

National Federation of State High School Athletic Associations. *Basketball Rules Book.* Elgin, Ill.: NFSHSAA.
Includes rules, rule interpretations, and standards for interscholastic competition.

National Collegiate Athletic Association. *Basketball Guide.* Shawnee Mission, Kans.: NCAA.
The official publication of the NCAA. Previews divisional and regional teams, schedules, and championships.

VISUAL AIDS

Women's Five-Player Basketball. 1973 Super 8, eight-loop series, silent, color. (McGraw-Hill, 1221 Avenue of the Americas, New York, NY 10020)
A West Coast team demonstrates dribbling techniques, driving, passing, shooting, rebounding, and blocking out.

Basketball. 1973 Super 8, nine-loop series, silent, color. (Scholastic Coach Athletic Series, 50 W. 44th St. N.W., New York, NY 10036)
Slow motion, stop action, and different angles are used to show dribbling, driving, passing, shooting, and rebounding techniques.

The Basketball Series. 1967 Super 8, 14-loop series, color, silent. (Athletic Institute, 200 N. Castlewood Dr., North Palm Beach, FL 33408)
Red Auerbach discusses major concerns in developing good fundamentals. Excellent for secondary school programs.

Basketball Conditioning Drills. 1968 15 min, sound, black and white, free loan. (Loan can be arranged through local Coca-Cola distributor)
John Wooden explains fundamental conditioning drills for practice sessions.

Fast Break. 15 min, sound, black and white. (Coca-Cola distributors)
Explanation of the fast break as demonstrated by the Ohio State University team.

Individual Defensive Skills. 9.5 min, sound, color. (Audiovisual Center, Division of Extension and University Services, University of Iowa, Iowa City, IA 52240)
Jerry West demonstrates balance, footwork, and total body movements to prevent the opponent from getting an open shot.

Basketball for Intermediate Grades. 27 min, sound, color. (Universal Education and Visual Arts, 221 Park Ave. S., New York, NY 10003)
Instructional techniques for teaching children in grades four through seven the fundamental skills.

The Jump Shot. 9 min 35 sec, sound, color (Sunkist Growers, P.O. Box 2706, Terminal Annex, Los Angeles, CA 90054)

Jerry West uses stop action and slow motion to demonstrate shooting technique for the jump shot.

Basketball Films. Series of five (18–20 min) 16mm or Super 8 instructional films, sound, color. (Amateur Athletic Union, 200 N. Castlewood Dr., North Palm Beach, FL 33408)

Features college all-stars as demonstrators. Titles include: "Techniques of Ball Handling," "Techniques of Shooting Handling," "Techniques of Offense Handling," "Techniques of Defense Handling," and "The Four Degrees of Defense."

Men's Basketball. Series of nine 8mm loops, silent. (Amateur Athletic Union)

Provides instruction on beginning and intermediate skills. Loops may be purchased singly or as a complete set. Topics include: "Speed and Control Dribble," "Crossover Change/Reverse Pivot Change," "Drive-Crossover-Drive," "Chest and Overhead Pass," "Lay-Up Shot," "Inside Power Shot," "Jump Shot," "Turnabout Jump Shot," and "Rebounding."

Women's Basketball. Series of eight 8mm loops, silent. (Amateur Athletic Union)

Beginning and intermediate skills as demonstrated by a women's collegiate team. Loops may be purchased singly or as a complete set. Topics include: "Basic, Control, and Speed Dribble," "Crossover/Reverse Dribble," "One-on-One Drives," "Chest/Bounce Pass," "Overarm/Overhead/Underhand Pass," "Lay-Up Shot," "Jump Shot/One-Hand Set Shot/Turnabout Jump Shot," and "Rebounding/Blocking Out."

Audio Cassettes

John Wooden Talking Basketball. Approx. 2 hr. (Amateur Athletic Union)

The legendary coach responds to questions regarding his coaching achievements, philosophy, and techniques.

Coach Billie Jean Moore Talking Basketball. (Amateur Athletic Union)

The Olympic and national championship coach offers teaching and coaching techniques.

Index

AAHPERD skills tests, 98-107
Affective scales, 118-119

Ball handling, 43-44
Baseball pass, 65-66
Bounce pass, 46-47

Catching, 44-45
Checklists, 110-111
Chest pass, 45-46
Circuit organization, 34-35
Coaching, 120-124
Coeducational play, 35-37
Conditioning, 13-27
Court dimensions, 6

Defenses
    individual, 59-62
    team, 85-87
Dribbling
    basic, 48-50
    change of pace, 69
    crossover, 69-71
    reverse, 71-72

Equipment, 8-12
Evaluation, 97-119
    charting statistics, 113-115
    rating scales, 110-111
    skill tests, 97-110
    written tests, 115-117

Facilities, 6-8, 9-10
Flip pass, 47-48
Floor surfaces, 6, 8
Footwork, 40-43, 60-61
Formations, 30-34
Free throws, 52-54

Grouping, 28

Handicapped adaptations, 37-38
Hook pass, 67

Hook shot, 74

Inverted lay-up, 72-73
Isometrics, 18-19
Isotonics, 18

Jump shot, 54-56

Lay-up shot, 50-52, 72-74
Lead-up games, 88-93

Modified equipment, 9-10
Modified games, 94-96

Objectives, 3-5
Offensive maneuvers. See Offensive patterns
Offensive patterns, 74-84
Organizing classes, 28
Out-of-bounds, 83-84

Passing, 45-48, 64-68
Philosophy, 3
Pivots, 41-43
Psychomotor tests, 97

Rebounding, 57-59
Relays, 93-94
Reverse lay-up, 73-74

Safety, 38
Shooting, 50-56, 72-74
Skills, teaching, 29
Stops, 41
Student leadership, 39

Teaching aids, 38
Team teaching, 29
Two-hand overhead pass, 67

Weight training, 19, 23, 23, 25-27

Zone defenses, 86